O

SERMON ON THE MOUNT

Our Lord's Sermon on the Mount

According to Matthew

by
St. Augustine of Hippo

TAN Books
Gastonia, North Carolina

This edition of *Our Lord's Sermon on the Mount* is from the edition published by T&T Clark, Edinburgh and Wm. B. Eerdmans Publishing Company, Grand Rapids, MI, 1945, translated by the Rev. William Findlay, MA, and revised by the Rev. D. S. Schaff. It was retypeset and published in 2025 by TAN Books.

Cover design by Caroline Green

Cover image: *Sermon on the Mount*, (detail) altarpiece in St. Matthew's Church, Copenhagen by Henrik Olrik. Public domain, via Wikimedia Commons.

ISBN: 978-1-5051-3563-3
Kindle ISBN: 978-1-5051-3565-7
ePUB ISBN: 978-1-5051-3564-0

Published in the United States by
TAN Books
PO Box 269
Gastonia, NC 28053
www.TANBooks.com

Printed in the United States of America

CONTENTS

BOOK I

*Explanation of the first part of the sermon
delivered by our Lord on the mount, as
contained in the fifth chapter of Matthew.*

BOOK II

*On the latter part of our Lord's Sermon on the Mount,
contained in the sixth and seventh chapters of Matthew.*

Book I

Explanation of the first part of the sermon delivered by our Lord on the mount, as contained in the fifth chapter of Matthew.

CHAPTER I

If any one will piously and soberly consider the sermon which our Lord Jesus Christ spoke on the mount, as we read it in the Gospel according to Matthew, I think that he will find in it, so far as regards the highest morals, a perfect standard of the Christian life: and this we do not rashly venture to promise, but gather it from the very words of the Lord Himself. For the sermon itself is brought to a close in such a way, that it is clear there are in it all the precepts which go to mould the life. For thus He speaks: "Therefore, whosoever heareth these words of mine, and doeth them, I will liken[1] him unto a wise man, which built his house upon a rock: and the rain descended, and the floods came, and the winds blew, and beat[2] upon that house; and it fell not: for it

---

[1] *Similabo*. The Vulgate, conforming more closely to the Greek, has *assimilabitur*, "shall be likened."

[2] *Offenderunt*; the Vulgate has *irruerunt*.

was founded upon a rock. And every one that heareth these words of mine, and doeth them not, I will liken[3] unto a foolish man, which built his house upon the sand: and the rain descended, and the floods came, and the winds blew, and beat upon that house; and it fell: and great was the fall of it." Since, therefore, He has not simply said, "Whosoever heareth my words," but has made an addition, saying, "Whosoever heareth these words of mine," He has sufficiently indicated, as I think, that these sayings which He uttered on the mount so perfectly guide the life of those who may be willing to live according to them, that they may justly be compared to one building upon a rock. I have said this merely that it may be clear that the sermon before us is perfect in all the precepts by which the Christian life is moulded; for as regards this particular section a more careful treatment will be given in its own place.[4]

---

3   The Vulgate, more closely conforming to the Greek, has *similis erit*.

4   The main purpose of the Sermon on the Mount has been variously stated. Augustine regards it as a perfect code of morals. Tholuck (*Die Bergpredigt*) calls it "the Magna Charta of the kingdom of heaven." Lange says, "The grand fundamental idea is to present the righteousness of the kingdom of heaven in its relation to that of the Old Testament theocracy." Geikie declares it to be the "formal inauguration of the kingdom of God and the Magna Charta

of our faith." Edersheim regards it as presenting "the full delineation of the ideal man of God, of prayer, and of righteousness; in short, of the inward and outward manifestation of discipleship." Meyer (*Com.* 6th ed. p. 210) says that the aim of Jesus is, as the One who fulfils the Law and the Prophets, to present the moral conditions of participation in the Messianic kingdom. Weiss *(Leben Jesu)* speaks of it as being "as little an ethical discourse as a new proclamation of law. It is nothing else than an announcement of the kingdom of God, in which is visible everywhere the purpose of Jesus to distinguish between its righteousness and the righteousness revealed in the Old Testament as well as that taught by the teachers of his day."

The Sermon on the Mount is a practical discourse, containing little of what, in the strict sense, may be termed the *credenda* of Christianity. It is the fullest statement of the nature and obligations of citizenship in God's kingdom. It is noteworthy for its omissions as well as for its contents. No reference is made to a priesthood, a ritual, sacred places, or offerings. There is almost a total absence of all that is sensuous and external. It deals with the motives and affections of the inner man, and so comes into comparison and contrast with the Mosaic law as well as with the Pharisaic ceremonialism of the Lord's Day. The moral grandeur of the precepts of the Sermon on the Mount has been acknowledged by believer and sceptics alike. Renan *(Life of Jesus)* says, "The Sermon on the Mount will never be surpassed." On the 15th of October, 1852, two weeks before he died, Daniel Webster wrote and signed his name to the following words, containing a testimony to this portion of Scripture, which he also ordered placed upon his tombstone: "Lord, I believe; help thou mine unbelief....My heart has assured me and reassured me that the gospel of Jesus Christ must

The beginning, then, of this sermon is introduced as follows: "And when He saw the great[5] multitudes,

---

be a divine reality. The Sermon on the Mount cannot be a merely human production. This belief enters into the very depth of my conscience. The whole history of man proves it" (Curtis, *Life of Webster*, ii. p. 684).

The relation which the reports of Matthew and Luke (vi. 20–49) sustain to each other is ignored by Augustine here (who, except in rare cases, omits all critical discussion), but is discussed in his *Harmony of the Gospels*, ii. 19. The agreements are numerous. The differences are striking, and concern the matter, the arrangement, the language, and the setting of the sermon. Matthew has a hundred and seven verses, Luke thirty. Matthew has seven (or eight) beatitudes, Luke but four, and adds four woes which Matthew omits. According to the first evangelist Jesus spoke sitting on a mountain: according to the third evangelist He spoke standing, and in the plain. The views are, (1) Matthew and Luke give accounts of the same discourse (Origen, Chrysostom, Calvin, Tholuck, Meyer, Keil, Schaff, Weiss). (2) They report different sermons spoken at different times (Augustine not positively, Storr, Plumptre). This is not probable, as so much of the matter in both is identical: both begin with the same beatitude, and close with the same parable; and both accounts are followed with the report of the healing of the centurion's servant. (3) The two sermons were delivered in close succession on the summit of the mountain to the disciples, and on the plain to the multitude (Lange). Alford confesses inability to reconcile the discrepancy.

5   *Multas turbas*. The Vulgate omits *multas*.

He went up into a mountain:[6] and when He was set, His disciples came unto Him: and He opened His mouth, and taught them, saying." If it is asked what the "mountain" means, it may well be understood as meaning the greater precepts of righteousness; for there were lesser ones which were given to the Jews. Yet it is one God who, through His holy prophets and servants, according to a thoroughly arranged distribution of times, gave the lesser precepts to a people who as yet required to be bound by fear; and who, through His Son, gave the greater ones to a people whom it had now become suitable to set free by love. Moreover,

---

6   The Greek has the definite article τὸ ὄρος. Some, on this ground, explain the expression to mean "mountain region." According to the Latin tradition of the time of the Crusaders, the exact spot is the Horns of Hattin, which Dean Stanley (*Sinai and Palestine*, Am. ed. p. 436) and most others adopt. The hill, which is horned like a saddle, is southwest of Capernaum, and commands a good view of the Lake of Galilee. It seems to meet the requirements of the text. Robinson says there are a dozen other hills as eligible as this one. Tholuck enlarges upon the "beautiful temple of nature in which the Lord delivered the sermon." Matthew Henry says, "When the law was given, the Lord came down upon the mountain, now the Lord went up; then He spake in thunder and lightning, now in a still, small voice; then the people were ordered to keep their distance, now they are invited to draw near,—a blessed change!"

when the lesser are given to the lesser, and the greater to the greater, they are given by Him who alone knows how to present to the human race the medicine suited to the occasion. Nor is it surprising that the greater precepts are given for the kingdom of heaven, and the lesser for an earthly kingdom, by that one and the same God, who made heaven and earth. With respect, therefore, to that righteousness which is the greater, it is said through the prophet, "Thy righteousness is like the mountains of God:"[7] and this may well mean that the one Master alone fit to teach matters of so great importance teaches on a mountain. Then He teaches sitting, as behooves the dignity of the instructor's office; and His disciples come to Him, in order that they might be nearer in body for hearing His words, as they also approached in spirit to fulfil His precepts. "And He opened His mouth, and taught them, saying." The circumlocution before us, which runs, "And He opened His mouth," perhaps gracefully intimates by the mere pause that the sermon will be somewhat longer than usual, unless, perchance, it should not be without meaning, that now He is said to have opened

---

7   Ps. xxxvi. 6.

His own mouth, whereas under the old law He was accustomed to open the mouths of the prophets.[8]

What, then, does He say? "Blessed are the poor in spirit, for theirs is the kingdom of heaven." We read in Scripture concerning the striving after temporal things, "All is vanity and presumption of spirit;"[9] but presumption of spirit means audacity and pride: usually also the proud are said to have great spirits; and rightly, inasmuch as the wind also is called spirit. And hence it is written, "Fire, hail, snow, ice, spirit of tempest."[10] But, indeed, who does not know that the proud are spoken of as puffed up, as if swelled out with wind? And hence also that expression of the apostle, "Knowledge puffeth up, but charity edifieth."[11] And "the poor in spirit" are rightly understood here, as meaning the humble and God-fearing, *i.e.* those who have not the spirit which puffeth up. Nor ought blessedness to begin at any other point whatever, if indeed it is to attain unto the highest

8   Chrysostom, Euthymius, etc., see in the expression the implication that Christ also taught by works. Tholuck, with many modern commentators, finds in it a reference to "loud and solemn utterance."

9   Eccles. i. 14.

10   Ps. cxlviii. 8.

11   1 Cor. viii. 1.

wisdom; "but the fear of the Lord is the beginning of wisdom;"[12] for, on the other hand also, "pride" is entitled "the beginning of all sin."[13] Let the proud, therefore, seek after and love the kingdoms of the earth; but "blessed are the poor in spirit, for theirs is the kingdom of heaven."[14]

---

12   Ps. cxi. 10.

13   Ecclesiasticus x. 13.

14   Not the intellectually poor (Fritzsche), nor the poor in worldly goods, as we might gather from Luke vi. 20. Roman Catholic commentators have found here support for the doctrine of voluntary poverty (Cornelius à Lapide, Maldonatus, etc.). The Emperor Julian, in allusion to this passage and others like it, said he would only confiscate the goods of Christians, that they might enter as *the poor* into the kingdom of heaven (*Lett.* xliii.). Some (Olearius, Michaelis, Paulus) have joined "in spirit" with "blessed." Augustine explains the passage of those who are not elated or proud, taking "spirit" in an evil sense. In another place he says, "Blessed are the poor in their own spirit, rich in God's Spirit, for every man who follows his own spirit is proud." He then compares him who subdues his own spirit to one living in a valley which is filled with water from the hills (*En. in Ps.* cxli. 4). The most explain of those who are conscious of spiritual need (Matt. xi. 28), and are ready to be filled with the gospel riches, as opposed to the spiritually proud, the just who need no repentance (Tholuck, Meyer, Lange, etc.). "Many are poor in the world, but high in spirit; poor and proud, murmuring and complaining, and blaming their lot. Laodicea was poor

in spirituals, and yet rich in spirit; so well increased with goods as to have need of nothing. Paul was rich in spirituals, excelling most in gifts and graces and yet poor in spirit; the least of the apostles, and less than the least of all saints" (M. Henry).

Chapter II

"Blessed are the meek, for they shall by inheritance possess[15] the earth:" that earth, I suppose, of which it is said in the Psalm, "Thou art my refuge, my portion in the land of the living."[16] For it signifies a certain firmness and stability of the perpetual inheritance, where the soul, by means of a good disposition, rests, as it were, in its own place, just as the body rests on the earth, and is nourished from it with its own food, as the body from the earth. This is the very rest and life of the saints. Then, the meek are those who yield to acts of wickedness, and do not resist evil, but overcome evil with good.[17] Let those, then, who are not meek quarrel and fight for earthly and temporal things; but "blessed

---

15 *Hereditate possidebunt.* Vulgate omits *hereditate*. The passage is quoted almost literally in the *Teaching of the Twelve Apostles*, iii. 7.
16 Ps. cxlii. 5.
17 Rom. xii. 21.

are the meek, for they shall by inheritance possess the earth," from which they cannot be driven out.[18]

"Blessed are they that mourn:[19] for they shall be comforted." Mourning is sorrow arising from the loss of things held dear; but those who are converted to God lose those things which they were accustomed to embrace as dear in this world: for they do not rejoice in those things in which they formerly rejoiced; and until the love of eternal things be in them, they are wounded by some measure of grief. Therefore they will be comforted by the Holy Spirit, who on this account chiefly

---

18 The order in which Augustine places this Beatitude is followed in *Cod.* D, and approved by Lachmann, Tischendorf, Neander, and others (not Westcott and Hort). The meek not only bear provocation, but quietly submit to God's dealings, and comply with His designs. The temporal possession promised is one of the few temporal promises in the New Testament. The inheritance of the earth is referred to "earthly good and possessions," by Chrysostom, Euthymius, Luther, etc.; to conquest of the world by the kingdom of God, by Neander, to the actual kingdom on this earth, first in its millennial then in its blessed state, by Alford; typically to the Messiah kingdom, by Meyer; to the land of the living beyond the heavens by Gregory of Nyssa. "Humility and meekness have been proved to be a conquering principle in the world's history" (Tholuck).

19 *Lugentes.* Greek, πενθοῦντες. The Vulgate, *qui lugent*, which Augustine follows, p. 7.

is called the Paraclete, *i.e.* the Comforter, in order that, while losing the temporal joy, they may enjoy to the full that which is eternal.[20]

"Blessed are they which do hunger and thirst after righteousness: for they shall be filled." Now He calls those parties, lovers of a true and indestructible good. They will therefore be filled with that food of which the Lord Himself says, "My meat is to do the will of my Father," which is righteousness; and with that water, of which whosoever "drinketh," as he also says, it "shall be in him a well of water, springing up into everlasting life."[21]

"Blessed are the merciful: for they shall obtain mercy."[22] He says that they are blessed who relieve the

---

20 The mourning is a mourning over sins of their own and others (Chrysostom, etc.); too restricted, as is also Augustine's explanation. Spiritual mourning in general (Ambrose, Jerome, Tholuck, etc.) sorrow according to God (2 Cor. vii. 10). We are helped to the meaning by comparing the woe on those that laugh (Luke vi. 22); that is, upon those who are satisfied with earthly things, and avoid the seriousness of repentance.

21 John iv. 34, 14.

22 *Ipsorum miserabitur*; closer to the Greek than the Vulgate *ipsi misericordiam consequentur*. The same thought that underlies the fifth petition of the Lord's Prayer, as Augustine also says, *Retract.* I. xix. 3.

miserable, for it is paid back to them in such a way that they are freed from misery.

"Blessed are the pure in heart:[23] for they shall see God." How foolish, therefore, are those who seek God with these outward eyes, since He is seen with the heart! as it is written elsewhere, "And in singleness of heart seek Him."[24] For that is a pure heart which is a single heart: and just as this light cannot be seen, except with pure eyes; so neither is God seen, unless that is pure by which He can be seen.[25]

"Blessed are the peacemakers: for they shall be called the children of God." It is the perfection of peace, where nothing offers opposition; and the children of God are peacemakers, because nothing resists

---

23   *Mundi corde*; the Vulgate, *mundo corde*.

24   Wisdom i. 1.

25   "Pure in heart." "Ceremonial purity does not suffice" (Bengel). The singleness of heart which has God's will for its aim, and follows integrity with our fellow men (Tholuck). "Shall see God:" the most infinite communion with God (Tholuck). The promise is fulfilled even here (Lange, Alford, Schaff, etc.). It concerns only the beatific vision in the spiritual body (Meyer). Not a felicity to the impure to see God (Henry). Comp. 1 John iii. 2, Rev. xxii. 4, etc. Augustine has a brilliant description of the future vision of God in *City of God* (*Nicene and Post-Nicene Fathers, Vol. ii.* pp. 507–509).

God, and surely children ought to have the likeness of their father. Now, they are peacemakers in themselves who, by bringing in order all the motions of their soul, and subjecting them to reason—*i.e.* to the mind and spirit—and by having their carnal lusts thoroughly subdued, become a kingdom of God: in which all things are so arranged, that that which is chief and pre-eminent in man rules without resistance over the other elements, which are common to us with the beasts; and that very element which is preeminent in man, *i.e.* mind and reason, is brought under subjection to something better still, which is the truth itself, the only begotten Son of God. For a man is not able to rule over things which are inferior, unless he subjects himself to what is superior. And this is the peace which is given on earth to men of goodwill;[26] this the life of the fully developed and perfect wise man. From a kingdom of this sort brought to a condition of thorough peace and order, the prince of this world is cast out, who rules where there is perversity and disorder.[27] When this

---

[26] Luke ii. 14.

[27] The "peacemakers" not only establish peace within themselves as Augustine, encouraged by the Latin word, explains, but diffuse peace around about them,—heal the alienations and discords of others, and bring about reconciliations in the world; not merely

peace has been inwardly established and confirmed, whatever persecutions he who has been cast out shall stir up from without, he only increases the glory which is according to God; being unable to shake anything in that edifice, but by the failure of his machinations making it to be known with how great strength it has been built from within outwardly. Hence there follows: "Blessed are they which are persecuted for righteousness' sake: for theirs is the kingdom of heaven."

---

peaceful, but peacemakers. "In most kingdoms those stand highest who make war: in the Messiah's kingdom the crowning beatitude respects those who make peace." The expressions will be remembered, "peace of God" (Phil. iv. 7); "peace of Christ" (Col. iii. 15); "God of peace" (Rom. xv. 33), etc. "If the peacemakers are blessed, woe to the peacebreakers!" (M. Henry).

CHAPTER III

There are in all, then, these eight sentences. For now in what remains He speaks in the way of direct address to those who were present, saying: "Blessed shall ye be when men shall revile you and persecute you." But the former sentences He addressed in a general way: for He did not say, Blessed are ye poor in spirit, for yours is the kingdom of heaven; but He says, "Blessed are the poor in spirit, for theirs is the kingdom of heaven:" nor, Blessed are ye meek, for ye shall inherit the earth; but, "Blessed are the meek, for they shall inherit the earth." And so the others up to the eighth sentence, where He says: "Blessed are they which are persecuted for righteousness' sake, for theirs is the kingdom of heaven." After that He now begins to speak in the way of direct address to those present, although what has been said before referred also to His present audience; and that which follows, and which seems to be spoken specially to those present, refers also to those who were absent, or who would afterwards come into existence.

For this reason the number of sentences before us is to be carefully considered. For the beatitudes begin with humility: "Blessed are the poor in spirit," *i.e.* those not puffed up, while the soul submits itself to divine authority, fearing lest after this life it go away to punishment, although perhaps in this life it might seem to itself to be happy. Then it (the soul) comes to the knowledge of the divine Scriptures, where it must show itself meek in its piety, lest it should venture to condemn that which seems absurd to the unlearned, and should itself be rendered unteachable by obstinate disputations. After that, it now begins to know in what entanglements of this world it is held by reason of carnal custom and sins: and so in this third stage, in which there is knowledge, the loss of the highest good is mourned over, because it sticks fast in what is lowest. Then, in the fourth stage there is labour, where vehement exertion is put forth, in order that the mind may wrench itself away from those things in which, by reason of their pestilential sweetness, it is entangled: here therefore righteousness is hungered and thirsted after, and fortitude is very necessary; because what is retained with delight is not abandoned without pain. Then, at the fifth stage, to those persevering in labour, counsel for getting rid of it is given; for unless each one is assisted by a superior, in no way is he fit in his own case to extricate himself from so great entanglements of miseries. But it is a just counsel, that he who wishes to be assisted by a stronger should assist him who is weaker in that in which he himself is stronger: therefore "blessed are the merciful, for they shall obtain mercy." At the sixth stage there is purity of heart, able from a good conscience of good works to contemplate that highest good, which can be discerned by the pure and tranquil intellect alone. Lastly is the seventh, wisdom itself—*i.e.* the contemplation of the truth, tranquillizing the whole man, and assuming the likeness of God, which is thus summed up: "Blessed are the peacemakers, for they shall be called the children of God." The eighth, as it were, returns to the starting point, because it shows and commends what is complete and perfect:[28] therefore in the first and in the eighth the kingdom of

---

28 "In the eighth beatitude the other seven are only summed up under the idea of the righteousness of the kingdom in its relation to those who persecute it; while the ninth is a description of the eighth, with reference to the relation in which these righteous persons stand to Christ" (Lange).

heaven is named, "Blessed are the poor in spirit, for theirs is the kingdom of heaven;" and, "Blessed are they which are persecuted for righteousness' sake, for theirs is the kingdom of heaven:" as it is now said, "Who shall separate us from the love of Christ? shall tribulation, or distress, or persecution, or famine, or nakedness, or peril, or sword?"[29] Seven in number, therefore, are the things which bring perfection: for the eighth brings into light and shows what is perfect, so that starting, as it were, from the beginning again, the others also are perfected by means of these stages.

---

29 Rom. viii. 35.

CHAPTER IV

Hence also the sevenfold operation of the Holy Ghost, of which Isaiah speaks,[30] seems to me to correspond to these stages and sentences. But there is a difference of order: for there the enumeration begins with the more excellent, but here with the inferior. For there it begins with wisdom, and closes with the fear of God: but "the fear of the Lord is the beginning of wisdom." And therefore, if we reckon as it were in a gradually ascending series, there the fear of God is first, piety second, knowledge third, fortitude fourth, counsel fifth, understanding sixth, wisdom seventh. The fear of God corresponds to the humble, of whom it is here said, "Blessed are the poor in spirit," *i.e.* those not puffed up, not proud: to whom the apostle says, "Be not

---

30   Isa. xi. 2, 3.

high minded, but fear;"[31] *i.e.* be not lifted up. Piety[32] corresponds to the meek: for he who inquires piously honours Holy Scripture, and does not censure what he does not yet understand, and on this account does not offer resistance; and this is to be meek: whence it is here said, "Blessed are the meek." Knowledge corresponds to those that mourn who already have found out in the Scriptures by what evils they are held chained which they ignorantly have coveted as though they were good and useful. Fortitude corresponds to those hungering and thirsting: for they labour in earnestly desiring joy from things that are truly good, and in eagerly seeking to turn away their love from earthly and corporeal things: and of them it is here said, "Blessed are they which do hunger and thirst after righteousness." Counsel corresponds to the merciful: for this is the one remedy for escaping from so great evils, that we forgive, as we wish to be ourselves forgiven; and that we assist others so far as we are able, as we ourselves desire to be assisted where we are not able: and of them it is here said, "Blessed are the merciful." Understanding corresponds to the pure in heart, the eye being as it were

---

31 Rom. xi. 20.

32 Augustine follows the Septuagint, which has "piety" instead of "the fear of the Lord" in the last clause of Isa. xi. 2.

purged, by which that may be beheld which eye hath not seen, nor ear heard, and what hath not entered into the heart of man:[33] and of them it is here said, "Blessed are the pure in heart." Wisdom corresponds to the peacemakers, in whom all things are now brought into order, and no passion is in a state of rebellion against reason, but all things together obey the spirit of man, while he himself also obeys God: and of them it is here said, "Blessed are the peacemakers."[34]

Moreover, the one reward, which is the kingdom of heaven, is variously named according to these stages. In the first, just as ought to be the case, is placed the kingdom of heaven, which is the perfect and highest wisdom of the rational soul. Thus, therefore, it is said, "Blessed are the poor in spirit, for theirs is the kingdom of heaven:" as if it were said, "The fear of the Lord is the beginning of wisdom." To the meek an inheritance is given, as it were the testament of a father to those dutifully seeking it: "Blessed are the meek, for they shall inherit the earth." To the mourners comfort, as to those who know what they have lost, and in what evils they are sunk: "Blessed are they that mourn, for they

---

33 Isa. lxiv. 4, 1 Cor. ii. 9.

34 This is guarded against misconstruction in the *Retract*. I. xix. 1.

shall be comforted." To those hungering and thirsting, a full supply, as it were a refreshment to those labouring and bravely contending for salvation: "Blessed are they which do hunger and thirst after righteousness, for they shall be filled." To the merciful mercy, as to those following a true and excellent counsel, so that this same treatment is extended toward them by one who is stronger, which they extend toward the weaker: "Blessed are the merciful, for they shall obtain mercy." To the pure in heart is given the power of seeing God, as to those bearing about with them a pure eye for discerning eternal things: "Blessed are the pure in heart, for they shall see God." To the peacemakers the likeness of God is given, as being perfectly wise, and formed after the image of God by means of the regeneration of the renewed man: "Blessed are the peacemakers, for they shall be called the children of God." And those promises can indeed be fulfilled in this life, as we believe them to have been fulfilled in the case of the apostles. For that all-embracing change into the angelic form, which is promised after this life, cannot be explained in any words. "Blessed," therefore, "are they which are persecuted for righteousness' sake, for theirs is the kingdom of heaven." This eighth sentence, which goes back to the starting point, and makes manifest the perfect man, is perhaps set forth in its meaning both by the circumcision on the eighth day in the Old Testament, and by the resurrection of the Lord after the Sabbath, the day which is certainly the eighth, and at the same time the first day; and by the celebration of the eight festival days which we celebrate in the case of the regeneration of the new man; and by the very number of Pentecost. For to the number seven, seven times multiplied, by which we make forty-nine, as it were an eighth is added, so that fifty may be made up, and we, as it were, return to the starting point: on which day the Holy Spirit was sent, by whom we are led into the kingdom of heaven, and receive the inheritance, and are comforted; and are fed, and obtain mercy, and are purified, and are made peacemakers; and being thus perfect, we bear all troubles brought upon us from without for the sake of truth and righteousness.

CHAPTER V

"Blessed are ye," says He, "when men shall revile you, and persecute you, and shall say all manner of evil against you falsely for my sake. Rejoice and be exceeding glad: for great[35] is your reward in heaven." Let any one who is seeking after the delights of this world and the riches of temporal things under the Christian name, consider that our blessedness is within; as it is said of the soul of the Church[36] by the mouth of the prophet, "All the beauty of the king's daughter is within;"[37] for outwardly revilings, and persecutions, and disparagements are promised; and yet, from these things there is a great reward in heaven, which is felt in the heart of those who endure, those who can now say, "We glory in tribulations: knowing that tribulation

---

35 *Multa*; Vulgate, *copiosa*.

36 *Anima ecclesiastica.*

37 Ps. xlv. 13.

worketh patience; and patience, experience; and experience, hope: and hope maketh not ashamed; because
the love of God is shed abroad in our hearts by the
Holy Ghost which is given unto us."[38] For it is not simply the enduring of such things that is advantageous,
but the bearing of such things for the name of Christ
not only with tranquil mind, but even with exultation.
For many heretics, deceiving souls under the Christian
name, endure many such things; but they are excluded
from that reward on this account, that it is not said
merely, "Blessed are they which endure persecution;"
but it is added, "for righteousness' sake." Now, where
there is no sound faith, there can be no righteousness,
for the just [righteous] man lives by faith.[39] Neither
let schismatics promise themselves anything of that
reward; for similarly, where there is no love, there cannot be righteousness, for "love worketh no ill to his
neighbour;"[40] and if they had it, they would not tear in
pieces Christ's body, which is the Church.[41]

But it may be asked, What is the difference when
He says, "when men shall revile you," and "when they

---

38   Rom. v. 3-5.
39   Hab. ii. 4, Rom. i. 17.
40   Rom. xiii. 10.
41   Col. i. 24.

shall say all manner of evil against you," since to revile[42] is just this, to say evil against?[43] But it is one thing when the reviling word is hurled with contumely in presence of him who is reviled, as it was said to our Lord, "Say we not the truth[44] that thou art a Samaritan, and hast a devil?"[45] and another thing, when our reputation is injured in our absence, as it is also written of Him, "Some said, He is a prophet;[46] others said, Nay, but He deceiveth the people."[47] Then, further, to persecute is to inflict violence, or to assail with snares, as was done by him who betrayed Him, and by them who crucified Him. Certainly, as for the fact that this also is not put in a bare form, so that it should be said, "and shall say all manner of evil against you," but there is added the word "falsely," and also the expression "for my sake;" I think that the addition is made for the sake of those who wish to glory in persecutions, and in the baseness of their reputation; and to say that Christ belongs to them for this reason, that many bad things are said

---

42 *Maledicere.*

43 *Malum dicere.*

44 *Verum.* The Vulgate more literally has *bene.*

45 John viii. 48.

46 The Vulgate, following the Greek, has *bonus,*—good man.

47 John vii. 12.

about them; while, on the one hand, the things said are true, when they are said respecting their error; and, on the other hand, if sometimes also some false charges are thrown out, which frequently happens from the rashness of men, yet they do not suffer such things for Christ's sake.[48] For he is not a follower of Christ who is not called a Christian according to the true faith and the catholic discipline.

"Rejoice," says He, "and be exceeding glad: for great is your reward in heaven." I do not think that it is the higher parts of this visible world that are here called heaven. For our reward, which ought to be immoveable and eternal, is not to be placed in things fleeting and temporal. But I think the expression "in heaven" means in the spiritual firmament, where dwells everlasting righteousness: in comparison with which a wicked soul is called earth, to which it is said when it sins, "Earth thou art, and unto earth thou shalt return."[49] Of this

---

48   "It is not the suffering but the cause, that makes men martyrs." For, says Augustine in another place (*En. in Ps.* xxxiv. 23), if the suffering made the martyr, every mine would be full of martyrs, every chain drag them, every one beheaded with the sword be crowned. They who suffer for righteousness' sake, suffer for Christ's sake.

49   Gen. iii. 19.

heaven the apostle says, "For our conversation is in heaven."[50] Hence they who rejoice in spiritual good are conscious of that reward now; but then it will be perfected in every part, when this mortal also shall have put on immortality. "For," says He, "so persecuted they the prophets also which were before you." In the present case He has used "persecution" in a general sense, as applying alike to abusive words and to the tearing in pieces of one's reputation; and has well encouraged them by an example, because they who speak true things are wont to suffer persecution: nevertheless did not the ancient prophets on this account, through fear of persecution, give over the preaching of the truth.

---

50 Phil. iii. 20.

Chapter VI

Hence there follows most justly the statement, "Ye are the salt of the earth;" showing that those parties are to be judged insipid, who, either in the eager pursuit after abundance of earthly blessings, or through the dread of want, lose the eternal things which can neither be given nor taken away by men. "But[51] if the salt have lost[52] its savour, wherewith shall it be salted?" *i.e.*, If ye, by means of whom the nations in a measure are to be preserved [from corruption], through the dread of temporal persecutions shall lose the kingdom of heaven, where will be the men through whom error may be removed from you, since God has chosen you, in order that through you He might remove the error of others? Hence the savourless salt is "good for nothing, but to be cast out, and trodden under foot of men." It

---

51 "A warning against pride" (Schaff).

52 *Infatuatum fuerit*; Vulgate, *evanuerit*.

is not therefore he who suffers persecution, but he who is rendered savourless by the fear of persecution, that is trodden under foot of men. For it is only one who is undermost that can be trodden under foot; but he is not undermost, who, however many things he may suffer in his body on the earth, yet has his heart fixed in heaven.[53]

---

53   Others follow Augustine in regarding the connection of this verse and the next with the preceding one as very close. All the more must they refuse to yield to persecution, as they have a function in the world which is well represented by salt and light (Weizsäcker, Meyer, etc.). The function of salt is to preserve and to season. With it Elisha healed the unwholesome water (2 Kings ii. 21). The use of salt in the sacrifices is, no doubt, alluded to (Tholuck). It becomes savourless. Dr. Thomson says (*Land and Book*, ii. 43), "It is a well known fact that the salt in this country (gathered from the marshes in dry weather), when in contact with the ground, or exposed to air and sun, does become insipid and useless." The disciples are appointed to communicate the truth and moral grace, before spoken of in the Beatitudes, to counteract the error and corruption in the earth. "Earth" not to be confined to "society as then existing, the definite form the world then presented" (Lange), but to mankind in general, as Augustine below. "Wherewith shall it be salted" does not imply that those who have once fallen cannot be reclaimed (Alford). The comment of Grotius is good: "*Ipsi emendare alios debebent, non autem exspectare ut ab aliis ipsi emendarentur*" ("They ought to improve others, not expect to be themselves improved by others").

"Ye are the light[54] of the world." In the same way as He said above, "the salt of the earth," so now He says, "the light of the world." For in the former case that earth is not to be understood which we tread with our bodily feet, but the men who dwell upon the earth, or even the sinners, for the preserving of whom and for the extinguishing of whose corruptions the Lord sent the apostolic salt. And here, by the world must be understood not the heavens and the earth, but the men who are in the world or love the world, for the enlightening of whom the apostles were sent.[55] "A city that is set on[56] an hill cannot be hid," *i.e.* [a city] founded upon great and distinguished righteousness, which is

---

54 *Lumen*, also used for a *luminary*; Vulgate, *lux*. In a lower and derivative sense are the disciples "the light," etc. (Alford), deriving their light-giving quality from Him who is the "Light of the world" (John viii. 12), so that they become "lights in the world" (Phil. ii. 15). Augustine (Sermon, ccclxxx.): *Johannes lumen illuminatum, Christus lumen illuminans.*

55 "The influence of salt is internal, of light external: hence the element in which they work, the *earth* and the *world*, both referring to mankind; the latter more to its organized external form" (Schaff).

56 *Constituta*; Vulgate, *posita*. The city was probably visible. Some have thought of the village on Mount Tabor, others of an ancient fortress, predecessor of the present Safed (Dean Stanley, Thomson); certainly not Jerusalem (Weizsäcker).

also the meaning of the mountain itself on which our Lord is discoursing. "Neither do men light a candle[57] and put it under a bushel measure."[58] What view are we to take? That the expression "under a bushel measure" is so used that only the concealment of the candle is to be understood, as if He were saying, No one lights a candle and conceals it? Or does the bushel measure also mean something, so that to place a candle under a bushel is this, to place the comforts of the body higher than the preaching of the truth; so that one does not preach the truth so long as he is afraid of suffering any annoyance in corporeal and temporal things? And it is well said a bushel measure, whether on account of the recompense of measure, for each one receives the things done in his body,—"that every one," says the apostle, "may there receive[59] the things done in his body;" and it is said in another place, as if of this bushel measure of the body, "For with what measure ye mete, it shall be measured to you again:"[60] —or because temporal good things, which are carried to completion in the

---

57 *Lucerna*.

58 The Greek has the definite article τὸν μόδιον.

59 2 Cor. v. 10. *Recipiat unusquisque quæ gessit in corpore*. Vulgate, *referat unusquisque propria corporis, prout gessit*, etc.

60 Matt. vii. 2.

body, are both begun and come to an end in a certain definite number of days, which is perhaps meant by the "bushel measure;" while eternal and spiritual things are confined within no such limit, "for God giveth not the Spirit by measure."[61] Every one, therefore, who obscures and covers up the light of good doctrine by means of temporal comforts, places his candle under a bushel measure. "But on a candlestick."[62] Now it is placed on a candlestick by him who subordinates his body to the service of God, so that the preaching of the truth is the higher, and the serving of the body the lower; yet by means even of the service of the body the doctrine shines more conspicuously, inasmuch as it is insinuated into those who learn by means of bodily functions, *i.e.* by means of the voice and tongue, and the other movements of the body in good works. The apostle therefore puts his candle on a candlestick, when he says, "So fight I, not as one that beateth[63] the air; but I keep under my body, and bring it into subjection, lest that by any means, when I preach to others, I myself

---

[61] John iii. 34; which words, however, are, as Augustine subsequently observed (*Retract*. I. xix. 3), applicable only to Christ.

[62] *Candelabrum*.

[63] *Cædens*; Vulgate, *verberans*.

should be found a castaway."[64] When He says, however, "that it may give light to all who are in the house," I am of opinion that it is the abode of men which is called a house, *i.e.* the world itself, on account of what He says before, "Ye are the light of the world;" or if any one chooses to understand the house as being the Church, this, too, is not out of place.

---

64 1 Cor. ix. 26, 27. *Ne forte aliis predicans…invenir.* Vulgate, *Ne forte cum aliis prædicaverim…efficir.*

CHAPTER VII

"Let your light,"[65] says He, "so shine before men, that they may see your good works, and glorify your Father which is in heaven." If He had merely said, "Let your light so shine before men, that they may see your good works," He would seem to have fixed an end in the praises of men, which hypocrites seek, and those who canvass for honours and covet glory of the emptiest kind. Against such parties it is said, "If I yet pleased men, I should not be the servant of Christ;"[66] and, by the prophet, "They who please men are put to shame, because God hath despised them;" and again, "God hath broken the bones of those who

---

65 *Lumen*; Vulgate, *lux*. Christ presupposes His righteousness to have become the principle of their life. "They were to stand forth openly and boldly with the message of the New Testament" (Lange).

66 Gal. i. 10.

41

please men;"[67] and again the apostle, "Let us not be desirous of vainglory;"[68] and still another time, "But let every man prove his own work, and then shall he have rejoicing in himself alone, and not in another."[69] Hence our Lord has not said merely, "that they may see your good works," but has added, "and glorify your Father who is in heaven:" so that the mere fact that a man by means of good works pleases men, does not there set it up as an end that he should please men; but let him subordinate this to the praise of God, and for this reason please men, that God may be glorified in him. For this is expedient for them who offer praise, that they should honour, not man, but God; as our Lord showed in the case of the man who was carried, where, on the paralytic being healed, the multitude, marvelling at His powers, as it is written in the Gospel, "feared and glorified God, which had given such power unto men."[70] And His imitator, the Apostle Paul, says, "But they had heard only, that he which persecuted us

---

67   Ps. liii. 5.
68   Gal. v. 26.
69   Gal. vi. 4.
70   Matt. ix. 8.

in times past now preacheth the faith which once he destroyed; and they glorified[71] God in me."

And therefore, after He has exhorted His hearers that they should prepare themselves to bear all things for truth and righteousness, and that they should not hide the good which they were about to receive, but should learn with such benevolence as to teach others, aiming in their good works not at their own praise, but at the glory of God, He begins now to inform and to teach them what they are to teach; as if they were asking Him, saying: Lo, we are willing both to bear all things for Thy name, and not to hide Thy doctrine; but what precisely is this which Thou forbiddest us to hide, and for which Thou commandest us to bear all things? Art Thou about to mention other things contrary to those which are written in the law? "No," says He; "for think not that I am come to destroy the law, or the prophets: I am not come to destroy, but to fulfil."

---

71 Gal. i. 23, 24. *Vastabat…glorificabant*; Vulgate, *expugnabat… clarificabant.*

CHAPTER VIII

I n this sentence the meaning is twofold.[72] We must
deal with it in both ways. For He who says, "I am not
come[73] to destroy the law, but to fulfil," means it either
in the way of adding what is wanting, or of doing what
is in it. Let us then consider that first which I have put
first: for he who adds what is wanting does not surely
destroy what he finds, but rather confirms it by perfecting it; and accordingly He follows up with the statement, "Verily I say unto you,[74] Till heaven and earth

---

[72] Here begins the second part of the Sermon. In it our Lord
sets forth His relation as a lawgiver to the Mosaic law, especially as
currently interpreted according to the letter only (Meyer, Alford
etc.).

[73] *Veni*; Greek, ἦλθον.

[74] A decisive assertion of authority. *Asseveratio gravissima ei propria, qui per se ipsum et per suam veritatem asseverat* (Bengel). The
prophet's most emphatic statement was, "Thus saith the Lord."
Christ speaks in His own name, as the fount of authority (John v.
20 and often: John iii. 3, John xiv. 12, etc.).

pass, one iota or one tittle shall in nowise pass from the law, till all be fulfilled." For, if even those things which are added for completion are fulfilled, much more are those things fulfilled which are sent in advance as a commencement. Then, as to what He says, "One iota or one tittle shall in nowise pass from the law," nothing else can be understood but a strong expression of perfection, since it is pointed out by means of single letters, among which letters "iota" is smaller than the others, for it is made by a single stroke; while a "tittle" is but a particle of some sort at the top of even that. And by these words He shows that in the law all the smallest particulars even are to be carried into effect.[75] After that He subjoins: "Whosoever, therefore, shall break one of these least commandments, and shall teach men so, he shall be called the least in the kingdom of heaven." Hence it is the least commandments that are meant by "one iota" and "one tittle." And therefore,

---

75   "Christ's words are decisive against all those who would set aside the Old Testament as without significance, or inconsistent with the New Testament" (Alford). Christ declares the New to be rooted in the Old; its consummation, not its destruction. The essence and purport of the law, the "whole law," was fulfilled by Him (Meyer). Theophylact well compares the law to a sketch, which Christ (like the painter) does not destroy, but fills out.

"whosoever shall break and shall teach [men] so,"—*i.e.* in accordance with what he breaks, not in accordance with what he finds and reads,—"shall be called the least in the kingdom of heaven;" and therefore, perhaps, he will not be in the kingdom of heaven at all, where only the great can be. "But whosoever shall do and teach [men] so,"[76]—*i.e.* who shall not break, and shall teach men so, in accordance with what he does not break,— "shall be called great in the kingdom of heaven." But in regard to him who shall be called great in the kingdom of heaven, it follows that he is also in the kingdom of heaven, into which the great are admitted: for to this what follows refers.

---

76   *Sic*; Greek, οὗτος; Vulgate, *hic*.

Chapter IX

"For I say unto you, that except your righteousness shall exceed the righteousness of the scribes and Pharisees, ye shall in no case enter into the kingdom of heaven;"[77] *i.e.*, unless ye shall fulfil not only those least precepts of the law which begin the man, but also those which are added by me, who am not come to destroy the law, but to fulfil it, ye shall not enter into the kingdom of heaven. But you say to me: If, when He was speaking above of those least commandments, He said that whosoever shall break one of them, and shall teach in accordance with his transgression,

---

77 "With all their care, they had not understood the true spirit of the law" (Schaff). The rest of the Sermon is largely a comment on this verse, Christ giving His interpretation of the law, and the righteousness following upon its observance; showing that the purport goes beyond the external act of obedience to the purpose of the heart, and that in the external act of obedience the real purport might be ignored.

49

is called the least in the kingdom of heaven; but that whosoever shall do them, and shall teach [men] so, is called great, and hence will be already in the kingdom of heaven, because he is great: what need is there for additions to the least precepts of the law, if he can be already in the kingdom of heaven, because whosoever shall do them, and shall so teach, is great? For this reason that sentence is to be understood thus: "But whosoever shall do and teach men so, the same shall be called great in the kingdom of heaven,"—*i.e.* not in accordance with those least commandments, but in accordance with those which I am about to mention. Now what are they? "That your righteousness," says He, "may exceed that of the scribes and Pharisees;" for unless it shall exceed theirs, ye shall not enter into the kingdom of heaven. Whosoever, therefore, shall break those least commandments, and shall teach men so, shall be called the least; but whosoever shall do those least commandments, and shall teach men so, is not necessarily to be reckoned great and meet for the kingdom of heaven; but yet he is not so much the least as the man who breaks them. But in order that he may be great and fit for that kingdom, he ought to do and teach as Christ now teaches, *i.e.* in order that his righteousness may exceed that of the scribes and Pharisees.

The righteousness of the Pharisees is, that they shall not kill; the righteousness of those who are destined to enter into the kingdom of God, that they be not angry without a cause. The least commandment, therefore, is not to kill; and whosoever shall break that, shall be called least in the kingdom of heaven; but whosoever shall fulfil that commandment not to kill, will not, as a necessary consequence, be great and meet for the kingdom of heaven, but yet he ascends a certain step. He will be perfected, however, if he be not angry without a cause; and if he shall do this, he will be much further removed from murder. For this reason he who teaches that we should not be angry, does not break the law not to kill, but rather fulfils it; so that we preserve our innocence both outwardly when we do not kill, and in heart when we are not angry.

"Ye have heard" therefore, says He, "that it was said to them of old time, Thou shalt not kill; and whosoever shall kill shall be in danger of the judgment. But I say unto you, that whosoever is angry with his brother without a cause[78] shall be in danger of the judgment: and whosoever shall say to his brother, Raca, shall be

---

78 *Sine causa.* The weight of critical evidence is against this clause, which is omitted by Tischendorf, Westcott, and Hort, the Vulgate and the Revised Version.

in danger of the council: but whosoever shall say, Thou fool, shall be in danger of the gehenna of fire." What is the difference between being in danger of the judgment, and being in danger of the council, and being in danger of the gehenna of fire?[79] For this last sounds most weighty, and reminds us that certain stages were passed over from lighter to more weighty, until the gehenna of fire was reached. And, therefore, if it is a lighter thing to be in danger of the judgment than to be in danger of the council, and if it is also a lighter thing to be in danger of the council than to be in danger of the gehenna of fire, we must understand it to be a lighter thing to be angry with a brother without a cause than to say "Raca;" and again, to be a lighter thing to say "Raca" than to say "Thou fool." For the danger would not have gradations, unless the sins also were mentioned in gradation.

But here one obscure word has found a place, for "Raca" is neither Latin nor Greek. The others, however,

---

79   The "judgment" (κρίσις) was the local court of seven, which every community was enjoined to have (Deut. xvi. 18). The "council" was the Sanhedrin, consisting of seventy-two members, sitting in Jerusalem. The "gehenna" was the vale of Hinnom, on the confines of Jerusalem, where sacrifices were offered to Moloch, and which became the place for refuse and the burning of dead bodies. In the New Testament it is equivalent to "hell."

are current in our language. Now, some have wished to derive the interpretation of this expression from the Greek, supposing that a ragged person is called "Raca," because a rag is called in Greek ῥάκος; yet, when one asks them what a ragged person is called in Greek, they do not answer "Raca;" and further, the Latin translator might have put the word *ragged* where he has placed "Raca," and not have used a word which, on the one hand, has no existence in the Latin language, and, on the other, is rare in the Greek. Hence the view is more probable which I heard from a certain Hebrew whom I had asked about it; for he said that the word does not mean anything, but merely expresses the emotion of an angry mind. Grammarians call those particles of speech which express an affection of an agitated mind *interjections*; as when it is said by one who is grieved, "Alas," or by one who is angry, "Hah." And these words in all languages are proper names, and are not easily translated into another language; and this cause certainly compelled alike the Greek and the Latin translators to put the word itself, inasmuch as they could find no way of translating it.[80]

---

80 *Raca* is from the Chald. אֵקֵיר, and is a term of contempt equivalent to empty-headed (Thayer's *Lexicon*). Trench translates, "Oh, vain man!"

There is therefore a gradation in the sins referred to, so that first one is angry, and keeps that feeling as a conception in his heart; but if now that emotion shall draw forth an expression of anger not having any definite meaning, but giving evidence of that feeling of the mind by the very fact of the outbreak wherewith he is assailed with whom one is angry, this is certainly more than if the rising anger were restrained by silence; but if there is heard not merely an expression of anger, but also a word by which the party using it now indicates and signifies a distinct censure of him against whom it is directed, who doubts but that this is something more than if merely an exclamation of anger were uttered? Hence in the first there is one thing, *i.e.* anger alone; in the second two things, both anger and a word that expresses anger; in the third three things, anger and a word that expresses anger, and in that word the utterance of distinct censure. Look now also at the three degrees of liability,—the judgment, the council, the gehenna of fire. For in the judgment an opportunity is still given for defence; in the council, however, although there is also wont to be a judgment, yet because the very distinction compels us to acknowledge that there is a certain difference in this place, the production of the sentence seems to belong to the council,

inasmuch as it is not now the case of the accused himself that is in question, whether he is to be condemned
or not, but they who judge confer with one another to
what punishment they ought to condemn him, who,
it is clear, is to be condemned; but the gehenna of fire
does not treat as a doubtful matter either the condemnation, like the judgment, or the punishment of him
who is condemned, like the council; for in the gehenna
of fire both the condemnation and the punishment of
him who is condemned are certain. Thus there are seen
certain degrees in the sins and in the liability to punishment;[81] but who can tell in what ways they are invisibly
shown in the punishments of souls? We are therefore to
learn how great the difference is between the righteousness of the Pharisees and that greater righteousness
which introduces into the kingdom of heaven, because
while it is a more serious crime to kill than to inflict
reproach by means of a word, in the one case killing

---

81   It is important "to keep in mind that there is no distinction in
kind between these punishments, only of *degree*. The 'judgment'
(κρίσις) inflicted death by the sword, the Sanhedrin death by
stoning, and the disgrace of the gehenna followed as an intensifi-
cation of death; but the punishment is one and the same,—*death*.
So also in the subject of the similitude. All the punishments are
spiritual; all result in *eternal death*, but with *various degrees*, as the
degrees of guilt have been" (Alford).

exposes one to the judgment, but in the other anger exposes one to the judgment, which is the least of those three sins; for in the former case they were discussing the question of murder among men, but in the latter all things are disposed of by means of a divine judgment, where the end of the condemned is the gehenna of fire. But whoever shall say that murder is punished by a more severe penalty under the greater righteousness if a reproach is punished by the gehenna of fire, compels us to understand that there are differences of gehennas.

Indeed, in the three statements before us, we must observe that some words are understood. For the first statement has all the words that are necessary. "Whosoever," says He, "is angry with his brother without a cause, shall be in danger of the judgment." But in the second, when He says, "and whosoever shall say to his brother, Raca," there is understood the expression *without cause*,[82] and thus there is subjoined, "shall be in danger of the council." In the third, now, where He says, "but whosoever shall say, Thou fool," two things are understood, both *to his brother* and *without cause*. And in this way we

---

82   Augustine helps us to understand how the word εἰκῆ (*without cause*) in the preceding clause crept into some of the Mss. In *Retract.* I. xix. 4 he makes the critical note and correction: "*Codices græci non habent sine causa.*"

defend the apostle when he calls the Galatians fools,[83] to whom he also gives the name of brethren; for he does not do it without cause. And here the word brother is to be understood for this reason, that the case of an enemy is spoken of afterwards, and how he also is to be treated under the greater righteousness.

---

83   Gal. iii. 1.

CHAPTER X

Next there follows here: "Therefore, if thou hast brought[84] thy gift to the altar, and there rememberest that thy brother hath ought against thee; leave there thy gift before the altar, and go thy way; first be reconciled to thy brother, and then come and offer thy gift." From this surely it is clear that what is said above is said of a brother: inasmuch as the sentence which follows is connected by such a conjunction that it confirms the preceding one; for He does not say, But if thou bring thy gift to the altar; but He says, "Therefore, if thou bring thy gift to the altar." For if it is not lawful to be angry with one's brother without a cause, or to say "Raca," or to say "Thou fool," much less is it lawful so to retain anything in one's mind, as that indignation may be turned into hatred. And to this belongs also what is said in another passage: "Let not

---

84   *Obtuleris*; Vulgate, *offers*.

the sun go down upon your wrath."[85] We are therefore commanded, when about to bring our gift to the altar, if we remember that our brother hath ought against us, to leave the gift before the altar, and to go and be reconciled to our brother, and then to come and offer the gift.[86] But if this is to be understood literally, one might perhaps suppose that such a thing ought to be done if the brother is present; for it cannot be delayed too long, since you are commanded to leave your gift before the altar. If, therefore, such a thing should come into your mind respecting one who is absent, and, as may happen, even settled down beyond the sea, it is absurd to suppose that your gift is to be left before the altar until you may offer it to God after having traversed both lands and seas. And therefore we are compelled to have recourse to an altogether internal and spiritual interpretation, in order that what has been said may be understood without absurdity.

And so we may interpret the altar spiritually, as being faith itself in the inner temple of God, whose

---

85   Eph. iv. 26.

86   The performance of an act of worship does not atone for an offence against a fellow man. The duties toward God never absolve from man's duties to his neighbour. *Inter rem sacram magis subit recordatio offensarum, quam in strepitu negotiorum* (Bengel).

emblem is the visible altar. For whatever offering we present to God, whether prophecy, or teaching, or prayer, or a psalm, or a hymn, and whatever other such like spiritual gift occurs to the mind, it cannot be acceptable to God, unless it be sustained by sincerity of faith, and, as it were, placed on that fixedly and immoveably, so that what we utter may remain whole and uninjured. For many heretics, not having the altar, *i.e.* true faith, have spoken blasphemies for praise; being weighed down, to wit, with earthly opinions, and thus, as it were, throwing down their offering on the ground. But there ought also to be purity of intention on the part of the offerer. And therefore, when we are about to present any such offering in our heart, *i.e.* in the inner temple of God ("For," as it is said, "the temple of God is holy, which temple ye are;"[87] and, "That Christ may dwell in the inner man[88] by faith in your hearts") if it occur to our mind that a brother hath ought against us, *i.e.* if we have injured him in anything (for then he has something against us whereas we have something against him if he has injured us, and in that case it is

---

[87] 1 Cor. iii. 17.

[88] Eph. iii. 17. *In interiore homine*, a different construction from the Greek, which has εἰς with the accusative. So Vulgate, *in interiorem hominem*.

not necessary to proceed to reconciliation: for you will not ask pardon of one who has done you an injury, but merely forgive him, as you desire to be forgiven by the Lord what you have committed against Him), we are therefore to proceed to reconciliation, when it has occurred to our mind that we have perhaps injured our brother in something; but this is to be done not with the bodily feet, but with the emotions of the mind, so that you are to prostrate yourself with humble disposition before your brother, to whom you have hastened in affectionate thought, in the presence of Him to whom you are about to present your offering. For thus, even if he should be present, you will be able to soften him by a mind free from dissimulation, and to recall him to goodwill by asking pardon, if first you have done this before God, going to him not with the slow movement of the body, but with the very swift impulse of love; and then coming, *i.e.* recalling your attention to that which you were beginning to do, you will offer your gift.[89]

But who acts in a way that he is neither angry with his brother without a cause, nor says "Raca" without a

---

89 "Discharge of duty to men does not absolve from duty to God." The passage has strong bearing upon the relation of morality and religion.

cause, nor calls him a fool without a cause, all of which are most proudly committed; or so, that, if perchance he has fallen into any of these, he asks pardon with suppliant mind, which is the only remedy; who but just the man that is not puffed up with the spirit of empty boasting? "Blessed" therefore "are the poor in spirit: for theirs is the kingdom of heaven." Let us look now at what follows.

CHAPTER XI

"Be kindly disposed,"[90] says he, "toward thine adversary quickly, whiles thou art in the way with him; lest at any time the adversary deliver thee to the judge, and the judge deliver thee to the officer, and thou be cast into prison. Verily I say unto thee, thou shalt by no means come out thence, till thou hast paid the uttermost farthing." I understand who the judge is: "For the Father judgeth no man, but hath committed all judgment unto the Son."[91] I understand who the officer is: "And angels," it is said, "ministered unto Him:"[92] and we believe that He will come with His angels to judge the quick and the dead. I understand

---

90 *Benevolus*; Vulgate, *consentiens*. What is matter of prudence in a civil case, becomes matter of life and death in spiritual things. The Lord does not intend to inculcate simply a law of worldly prudence as asserted by a few modern commentators.

91 John v. 22.

92 Matt. iv. 11.

what is meant by the prison: evidently the punishments of darkness, which He calls in another passage the outer darkness:[93] for this reason, I believe, that the joy of the divine rewards is something internal in the mind itself, or even if anything more hidden can be thought of, that joy of which it is said to the servant who deserved well, "Enter thou into the joy of thy Lord;"[94] just as also, under this republican government, one who is thrust into prison is sent out from the council chamber, or from the palace of the judge.

But now, with respect to paying the uttermost farthing,[95] it may be understood without absurdity either as standing for this, that nothing is left unpunished; just as in common speech we also say "to the very dregs," when we wish to express that something is so drained out that nothing is left: or by the expression "the uttermost farthing" earthly sins may be meant. For as a fourth part of the separate component parts of this world, and in fact as the last, the earth is found; so that you begin with the heavens, you reckon the air the second, water the third,

---

93 Matt. viii. 12.

94 Matt. xxv. 23.

95 The word translated "farthing" means literally "a fourth part" and on this original sense Augustine's second interpretation is based.

the earth the fourth. It may therefore seem to be suitably said, "till thou hast paid the last fourth," in the sense of "till thou hast expiated thy earthly sins:" for this the sinner also heard, "Earth thou art, and unto earth shall thou return."[96] Then, as to the expression "till thou hast paid," I wonder if it does not mean that punishment which is called eternal.[97] For whence is that debt paid where there is now no opportunity given of repenting and of leading a more correct life? For perhaps the expression "till thou hast paid" stands here in the same sense as in that passage where it is said, "Sit Thou at my right hand, until I make Thine enemies Thy footstool;"[98] for not even when the enemies have been put under His feet, will He cease to sit at the right hand: or that statement of the apostle, "For He must reign, till He hath put all enemies under His feet;"[99] for not even when they have been put under

---

96 Gen. iii. 19.

97 Universalists have quoted the passage to prove the doctrine that punishment will not be endless, others in favor of purgatory. The main idea is the inexorable rigor of the divine justice against the impenitent. "The whole tone of the passage is that of one who seeks to deepen the sense of danger, not to make light of it; to make men feel that they cannot pay their debt, though God may forgive it freely" (Plumptre).

98 Ps. cx. 1.

99 1 Cor. xv. 25.

His feet, will He cease to reign. Hence, as it is there understood of Him respecting whom it is said, "He must reign, till He hath put His enemies under His feet," that He will reign for ever, inasmuch as they will be for ever under His feet: so here it may be understood of him respecting whom it is said, "Thou shalt by no means come out thence, till thou hast paid the uttermost farthing," that he will never come out; for he is always paying the uttermost farthing, so long as he is suffering the everlasting punishment of his earthly sins. Nor would I say this in such a way as that I should seem to prevent a more careful discussion respecting the punishment of sins, as to how in the Scriptures it is called eternal; although in all possible ways it is to be avoided rather than known.

But let us now see who the adversary himself is, with whom we are enjoined to agree quickly, whiles we are in the way with him. For he is either the devil, or a man, or the flesh, or God, or His commandment.[100] But I do not see how we should be enjoined to be on terms of goodwill, *i.e.* to be of one heart or of one mind, with the devil. For some have rendered the Greek word which is found here "of one heart," others

---

100 "The devil" (Clemens Alex.); "conscience" (Euthymius, Zig.); "the man who has done the injury" (Meyer, Tholuck, Lange, Trench, etc.)

"of one mind:" but neither are we enjoined to show goodwill to the devil (for where there is goodwill there is friendship: and no one would say that we are to make friends with the devil); nor is it expedient to come to an agreement with him, against whom we have declared war by once for all renouncing him, and on conquering whom we shall be crowned; nor ought we now to yield to him, for if we had never yielded to him, we should never have fallen into such miseries. Again, as to the adversary being a man, although we are enjoined to live peaceably with all men, as far as lieth in us, where certainly goodwill, and concord, and consent may be understood; yet I do not see how I can accept the view, that we are delivered to the judge by a man, in a case where I understand Christ to be the judge, "before" whose "judgment seat we must all appear,"[101] as the apostle says: how then is he to deliver me to the judge, who will appear equally with me before the judge? Or if any one is delivered to the judge because he has injured a man, although the party who has been injured does not deliver him, it is a much more suitable view, that the guilty party is delivered to the judge by that law against which he acted when he injured the man.

---

[101] 2 Cor. v. 10. *Exhiberi*; Vulgate, *manifestari*.

And this for the additional reason, that if any one has injured a man by killing him, there will be no time now in which to agree with him; for he is not now in the way with him, *i.e.* in this life: and yet a remedy will not on that account be excluded, if one repents and flees for refuge with the sacrifice of a broken heart to the mercy of Him who forgives the sins of those who turn to Him, and who rejoices more over one penitent than over ninety-nine just persons.[102] But much less do I see how we are enjoined to bear goodwill towards, or to agree with, or to yield to, the flesh. For it is sinners rather who love their flesh, and agree with it, and yield to it; but those who bring it into subjection are not the parties who yield to it, but rather they compel it to yield to them.

Perhaps, therefore, we are enjoined to yield to God, and to be well-disposed towards Him, in order that we may be reconciled to Him, from whom by sinning we have turned away, so that He can be called our adversary. For He is rightly called the adversary of those whom He resists, for "God resisteth the proud, but giveth grace to the humble;"[103] and "pride is the beginning of all sin, but the beginning of man's pride is to become apostate from

---

102 Luke xv. 7.
103 Jas. iv. 6.

God;"[104] and the apostle says, "For if, when we were enemies, we were reconciled to God by the death of His Son,
much more, being reconciled, we shall be saved by His
life."[105] And from this it may be perceived that no nature
[as being] bad is an enemy to God, inasmuch as the very
parties who were enemies are being reconciled. Whoever, therefore, while in this way, *i.e.* in this life, shall not
have been reconciled to God by the death of His Son,
will be delivered to the judge by Him, for "the Father
judgeth no man, but hath delivered all judgment to the
Son;" and so the other things which are described in this
section follow, which we have already discussed. There is
only one thing which creates a difficulty as regards this
interpretation, viz. how it can be rightly said that we are
in the way with God, if in this passage He Himself is
to be understood as the adversary of the wicked, with
whom we are enjoined to be reconciled quickly; unless,
perchance, because He is everywhere, we also, while we
are in this way, are certainly with Him. For as it is said,
"If I ascend up into heaven, Thou art there; if I make my
bed in hell, behold, Thou art there. If I take the wings
of the morning, and dwell in the uttermost parts of the
sea; even there shall Thy hand lead me, and Thy right

104 Sir. x. 13, 12.
105 Rom. v. 10.

hand shall hold me."[106] Or if the view is not accepted,
that the wicked are said to be with God, although there
is nowhere where God is not present,—just as we do not
say that the blind are with the light, although the light
surrounds their eyes,—there is one resource remaining:
that we should understand the adversary here as being
the commandment of God. For what is so much an adversary to those who wish to sin as the commandment of
God, *i.e.* His law and divine Scripture, which has been
given us for this life, that it may be with us in the way,
which we must not contradict, lest it deliver us to the
judge, but which we ought to submit to quickly? For no
one knows when he may depart out of this life. Now,
who is it that submits to divine Scripture, save he who
reads or hears it piously, deferring to it as of supreme
authority; so that what he understands he does not hate
on this account, that he feels it to be opposed to his sins,
but rather loves being reproved by it, and rejoices that
his maladies are not spared until they are healed; and
so that even in respect to what seems to him obscure or
absurd, he does not therefore raise contentious contra-
dictions, but prays that he may understand, yet remem-
bering that goodwill and reverence are to be manifested

106 Ps. cxxxix. 8-10.

towards so great an authority? But who does this, unless just the man who has come, not harshly threatening, but in the meekness of piety, for the purpose of opening and ascertaining the contents of his father's will? "Blessed," therefore, "are the meek: for they shall inherit the earth." Let us see what follows.

Chapter XII

"Ye have heard that it was said to them of old time, Thou shalt not commit adultery: but I say unto you, that whosoever looketh on a woman to lust after her, hath committed adultery with her already in his heart." The lesser righteousness, therefore, is not to commit adultery by carnal connection; but the greater righteousness of the kingdom of God is not to commit adultery in the heart. Now, the man who does not commit adultery in the heart, much more easily guards against committing adultery in actual fact. Hence He who gave the later precept confirmed the earlier; for He came not to destroy the law, but to fulfil it. It is well worthy of consideration that He did not say, "Whosoever lusteth after a woman," but, "Whosoever looketh on a woman to lust after her,"[107] *i.e.* turneth toward her

---

107 The Greek πρὸς τὸ ἐπιθυμῆσαι refers to sin of intent. "The particle πρός indicates the mental aim" (Tholuck, Meyer, etc.). So

with this aim and this intent, that he may lust after her;
which, in fact, is not merely to be tickled[108] by fleshly
delight, but fully to consent to lust; so that the forbidden appetite is not restrained, but satisfied if opportunity should be given.

For there are three things which go to complete
sin: the suggestion of, the taking pleasure in, and the
consenting to. Suggestion takes place either by means
of memory, or by means of the bodily senses, when
we see, or hear, or smell, or taste, or touch anything.
And if it give us pleasure to enjoy this, this pleasure,
if illicit, must be restrained. Just as when we are fasting, and on seeing food the appetite of the palate is
stirred up, this does not happen without pleasure; but
we do not consent to this liking, and[109] we repress
it by the right of reason, which has the supremacy.
But if consent shall take place, the sin will be complete, known to God in our heart, although it may
not become known to men by deed. There are, then,
these steps: the suggestion is made, as it were, by a
serpent, that is to say, by a fleeting and rapid, *i.e.* a
temporary, movement of bodies: for if there are also

Augustine, rightly: "Qui *hoc fine et hoc animo* attenderit."
108 *Titillari.*
109 The reading "if" has been proposed by some.

any such images moving about in the soul, they have been derived from without from the body; and if any hidden sensation of the body besides those five senses touches the soul, that also is temporary and fleeting; and therefore the more clandestinely it glides in, so as to affect the process of thinking, the more aptly is it compared to a serpent. Hence these three stages, as I was beginning to say, resemble that transaction which is described in Genesis, so that the suggestion and a certain measure of suasion is put forth, as it were, by the serpent; but the taking pleasure in it lies in the carnal appetite, as it were in Eve; and the consent lies in the reason, as it were in the man: and these things having been acted through, the man is driven forth, as it were, from paradise, *i.e.* from the most blessed light of righteousness, into death[110] —in all respects most righteously. For he who puts forth suasion does not compel. And all natures are beautiful in their order, according to their gradations; but we must not descend from the higher, among which the rational mind has its place assigned, to the lower. Nor is any one compelled to do this; and therefore, if he does it, he is punished by the just law of God, for he is not

---

110 Gen. iii.

guilty of this unwillingly. But yet, previous to habit, either there is no pleasure, or it is so slight that there is hardly any; and to yield to it is a great sin, as such pleasure is unlawful. Now, when any one does yield, he commits sin in the heart. If, however, he also proceeds to action, the desire seems to be satisfied and extinguished; but afterwards, when the suggestion is repeated, a greater pleasure is kindled, which, however, is as yet much less than that which by continuous practice is converted into habit. For it is very difficult to overcome this; and yet even habit itself, if one does not prove untrue to himself, and does not shrink back in dread from the Christian warfare, he will get the better of under His (*i.e.* Christ's) leadership and assistance; and thus, in accordance with primitive peace and order, both the man is subject to Christ, and the woman is subject to the man.[111]

Hence, just as we arrive at sin by three steps,—suggestion, pleasure, consent,—so of sin itself there are three varieties,—in heart, in deed, in habit,—as it were, three deaths: one, as it were, in the house, *i.e.* when we consent to lust in the heart; a second now, as it were, brought forth outside the gate, when assent goes forward

---

111 1 Cor. xi. 3, Eph. v. 23.

into action; a third, when the mind is pressed down by the force of bad habit, as if by a mound of earth, and is now, as it were, rotting in the sepulchre. And whoever reads the Gospel perceives that our Lord raised to life these three varieties of the dead. And perhaps he reflects what differences may be found in the very word of Him who raises them, when He says on one occasion, "Damsel, arise;"[112] on another, "Young man,[113] I say unto thee, Arise;"[114] and when on another occasion He groaned in the spirit, and wept, and again groaned, and then afterwards "cried with a loud voice, Lazarus, come forth."[115]

And therefore, under the category of the adultery mentioned in this section, we must understand all fleshly and sensual lust. For when Scripture so constantly speaks of idolatry as fornication, and the Apostle Paul calls avarice by the name of idolatry,[116] who doubts but that every evil lust is rightly called fornication, since the soul, neglecting the higher law by which it is ruled, and prostituting itself for the base pleasure of the lower nature as its reward (so to speak),

---

112 Mark v. 41.

113 *Juvenis*; Vulgate, *adolescens*.

114 Luke vii. 14.

115 John xi. 33-44.

116 Col. iii. 5, Eph. v. 5.

is thereby corrupted? And therefore let every one who feels carnal pleasure rebelling against right inclination in his own case through the habit of sinning, by whose unsubdued violence he is dragged into captivity, recall to mind as much as he can what kind of peace he has lost by sinning, and let him cry out, "O wretched man that I am! who shall deliver me from the body of this death? I thank God through Jesus Christ."[117] For in this way, when he cries out that he is wretched, in the act of bewailing he implores the help of a comforter. Nor is it a small approach to blessedness, when he has come to know his wretchedness; and therefore "blessed" also "are they that mourn,[118] for they shall be comforted."

---

117 Rom. vii. 24, 25.
118 *Lugentes*; Vulgate, *qui lugent*.

CHAPTER XIII

In the next place, He goes on to say: "And if thy right eye offend thee, pluck it out, and cast it from thee: for it is profitable for thee that one of thy members should perish, and not that thy whole body should go[119] into hell." Here, certainly, there is need of great courage in order to cut off one's members.[120] For whatever it is that is meant by the "eye," undoubtedly it is such a thing as is ardently loved. For those who wish to express their affection strongly are wont to speak thus: I love him as my own eyes, or even more than my own eyes. Then, when the word "right" is added, it is meant perhaps to intensify the strength of the affection.[121] For

---

119 *Eat*; Vulgate, *mittatur.*

120 Not literally (Fritzsche). Excision of the members would not of itself destroy the lust of the heart.

121 So Meyer *et al.* What Robert South says (*Sermon* on John vii. 17) of the Sermon on the Mount as a whole, can certainly be applied here: "All the particulars of Matt. v.-vii. are wrapt up

although these bodily eyes of ours are turned in a common direction for the purpose of seeing, and if both are turned they have equal power, yet men are more afraid of losing the right one. So that the sense in this case is: Whatever it is which thou so lovest that thou reckonest it as a right eye, if it offends thee, *i.e.* if it proves a hindrance to thee on the way to true happiness, pluck it out and cast it from thee. For it is profitable for thee, that one of these which thou so lovest that they cleave to thee as if they were members, should perish, rather than that thy whole body should be cast into hell.

But since He follows it up with a similar statement respecting the right hand, "If thy right hand offend thee, cut it off, and cast it from thee: for it is profitable for thee that one of thy members should perish, and not that thy whole body should go[122] into hell," He compels us to inquire more carefully what He has

---

in the doctrine of self-denial, prescribing to the world the most inward purity of heart, and a constant conflict with all our sensual appetites and worldly interests," etc. Augustine's interpretation is correct as far as it goes, but it is too restricted. Christ does not here insist upon the renunciation of sinful lusts, but upon the evasion of occasions of sin. What is harmless and innocent of itself, when through any temperament or condition it becomes an occasion of sinning, is to be relinquished.

122 *Eat*. So Vulgate.

spoken of as an eye. And as regards this inquiry, nothing occurs to me as a more suitable explanation than a greatly beloved friend: for this, certainly, is something which we may rightly call a member which we ardently love; and this friend a counsellor, for it is an eye, as it were, pointing out the road; and that in divine things, for it is the right eye: so that the left is indeed a beloved counsellor, but in earthly matters, pertaining to the necessities of the body; concerning which as a cause of stumbling it was superfluous to speak, inasmuch as not even the right was to be spared. Now, a counsellor in divine things is a cause of stumbling, if he endeavours to lead one into any dangerous heresy under the guise of religion and doctrine. Hence also let the right hand be taken in the sense of a beloved helper and assistant in divine works: for in like manner as contemplation is rightly understood as having its seat in the eye, so action in the right hand; so that the left hand may be understood in reference to works which are necessary for this life, and for the body.

Chapter XIV

"It hath been said, Whosoever shall put away his wife, let him give her a writing of divorcement." This is the lesser righteousness of the Pharisees, which is not opposed by what our Lord says: "But I say unto you, That whosoever shall put away his wife, saving for the cause of fornication, causeth her to commit adultery:[123] and whosoever shall marry her that is loosed from her husband committeth adultery."[124] For He who gave the commandment that a writing of divorcement should be given, did not give the commandment that a wife should be put away; but "whosoever shall put away," says He, "let him give her a writing of divorcement," in order that the thought of such a writing might

---

[123] *Per alias nuptias, quarum potestatem dat divortium* ("by another marriage, power of which divorce gives."—Bengel). So also Meyer, Alford, etc.

[124] *Solutam a viro…moechatur*; Vulgate, *dimissam…adulterat.*

moderate the rash anger of him who was getting rid of his wife. And, therefore, He who sought to interpose a delay in putting away, indicated as far as He could to hard-hearted men that He did not wish separation. And accordingly the Lord Himself in another passage, when a question was asked Him as to this matter, gave this reply: "Moses did so because of the hardness of your hearts."[125] For however hard-hearted a man may be who wishes to put away his wife, when he reflects that, on a writing of divorcement being given her, she could then without risk marry another, he would be easily appeased. Our Lord, therefore, in order to confirm that principle, that a wife should not lightly be put away, made the single exception of fornication; but enjoins that all other annoyances, if any such should happen to spring up, be borne with fortitude for the sake of conjugal fidelity and for the sake of chastity; and he also calls that man an adulterer who should marry her that has been divorced by her husband. And the Apostle Paul shows the limit of this state of affairs, for he says it is to be observed as long as her husband liveth; but on the husband's death he gives permission to marry.[126] For he himself also held by this rule, and

---

125 Matt. xix. 8.
126 Rom. vii. 2, 3.

therein brings forward not his own advice, as in the case of some of his admonitions, but a command by the Lord when he says: "And unto the married[127] I command, yet not I, but the Lord, Let not the wife[128] depart from her husband: but and if she depart, let her remain unmarried, or be reconciled to her husband: and let not the husband put away his wife."[129] I believe that, according to a similar rule, if he shall put her away, he is to remain unmarried, or be reconciled to his wife. For it may happen that he puts away his wife for the cause of fornication, which our Lord wished to make an exception of. But now, if she is not allowed to marry while the husband is living from whom she has departed, nor he to take another while the wife is living whom he has put away, much less is it right to commit unlawful acts of fornication with any parties whomsoever. More blessed indeed are those marriages to be reckoned, where the parties concerned, whether after the procreation of children, or even through contempt of such an earthly progeny, have been able with common consent to practise self-restraint toward each other: both because nothing is done contrary to that

---

127 *In conjugio…mulierem*; Vulgate, *matrimonio…uxorem.*
128 *In conjugio…mulierem*; Vulgate, *matrimonio…uxorem.*
129 1 Cor. vii. 10, 11.

precept whereby the Lord forbids a spouse to be put away (for he does not put her away who lives with her not carnally, but spiritually), and because that principle is observed to which the apostle gives expression, "It remaineth, that they that have wives be as though they had none."[130]

---

130 1 Cor. vii. 29.

Chapter XV

But it is rather that statement which the Lord Himself makes in another passage which is wont to disturb the minds of the little ones, who nevertheless earnestly desire to live now according to the precepts of Christ: "If any man come to me, and hate not his father, and mother, and wife, and children, and brethren, and sisters, yea, and his own life also, he cannot be my disciple."[131] For it may seem a contradiction to the less intelligent, that here He forbids the putting away of a wife saving for the cause of fornication, but that elsewhere He affirms that no one can be a disciple of His who does not hate his wife. But if He were speaking with reference to sexual intercourse, He would not place father, and mother, and brothers in the same category. But how true it is, that "the kingdom of heaven suffereth violence, and they that use violence

---

131 Luke xiv. 26.

take it by force!"[132] For how great violence is necessary, in order that a man may love his enemies, and hate his father, and mother, and wife, and children, and brothers! For He commands both things who calls us to the kingdom of heaven. And how these things do not contradict each other, it is easy to show under His guidance; but after they have been understood, it is difficult to carry them out, although this too is very easy when He Himself assists us. For in that eternal kingdom to which He has vouchsafed to call His disciples, to whom He also gives the name of brothers, there are no temporal relationships of this sort. For "there is neither Jew nor Greek, there is neither bond nor free, there is neither male nor female;" "but Christ is all, and in all."[133] And the Lord Himself says: "For in the resurrection they neither marry, nor are given in marriage,[134] but are as the angels of God in heaven."[135] Hence it is necessary that whoever wishes here and now to aim after the life of that kingdom, should hate not the persons themselves, but those temporal relationships by which this life of ours, which is transitory and is

---

132 Matt xi. 12. *Qui vim faciunt diripiunt illud*; Vulgate, *violenti rapiunt illud*.

133 Gal. iii. 28, Col. iii. 11.

134 *Uxores ducent*; Vulgate, *nubentur*.

135 Matt. xxii. 30.

comprised in being born and dying, is upheld; because he who does not hate them, does not yet love that life where there is no condition of being born and dying, which unites parties in earthly wedlock.

Therefore, if I were to ask any good Christian who has a wife, and even though he may still be having children by her, whether he would like to have his wife in that kingdom; mindful in any case of the promises of God, and of that life where this incorruptible shall put on incorruption, and this mortal shall put on immortality;[136] though at present hesitating from the greatness, or at least from a certain degree of love, he would reply with execration that he is strongly averse to it. Were I to ask him again, whether he would like his wife to live with him there, after the resurrection, when she had undergone that angelic change which is promised to the saints, he would reply that he desired this as strongly as he reprobated the other. Thus a good Christian is found in one and the same woman to love the creature of God, whom he desires to be transformed and renewed; but to hate the corruptible and mortal conjugal connection and sexual intercourse: *i.e.* to love in her what is characteristic of a human being, to hate what belongs to her as

---

136 1 Cor. xv. 53, 54.

a wife. So also he loves his enemy, not in as far as he is
an enemy, but in as far as he is a man; so that he wishes
the same prosperity to come to him as to himself, viz.
that he may reach the kingdom of heaven rectified and
renewed. This is to be understood both of father and
mother and the other ties of blood, that we hate in them
what has fallen to the lot of the human race in being
born and dying, but that we love what can be carried
along with us to those realms where no one says, My
Father; but all say to the one God, "Our Father:" and no
one says, My mother; but all say to that other Jerusalem,
Our mother: and no one says, My brother; but each says
respecting every other, Our brother. But in fact there will
be a marriage on our part as of one spouse (when we
have been brought together into unity), with Him who
hath delivered us from the pollution of this world by
the shedding of His own blood. It is necessary, therefore,
that the disciple of Christ should hate these things which
pass away, in those whom he desires along with himself
to reach those things which shall for ever remain; and
that he should the more hate these things in them, the
more he loves themselves.

A Christian may therefore live in concord with his
wife, whether with her providing for a fleshly craving,
a thing which the apostle speaks by permission, not

by commandment; or providing for the procreation of children, which may be at present in some degree praiseworthy; or providing for a brotherly and sisterly fellowship, without any corporeal connection, having his wife as though he had her not, as is most excellent and sublime in the marriage of Christians: yet so that in her he hates the name of temporal relationship, and loves the hope of everlasting blessedness. For we hate, without doubt, that respecting which we wish at least, that at some time hereafter it should not exist; as, for instance, this same life of ours in the present world, which if we were not to hate as being temporal, we would not long for the future life, which is not conditioned by time. For as a substitute for this life the soul is put, respecting which it is said in that passage, "If a man hate not his own soul[137] also, he cannot be my disciple." For that corruptible meat is necessary for this life, of which the Lord Himself says, "Is not the soul[138] more than meat?" *i.e.* this life to which meat is necessary. And when He says that He would lay down His soul[139] for His sheep, He undoubtedly means this life, as He is declaring that He is going to die for us.

---

137 Luke xiv. 26.

138 Matt. vi. 25.

139 John x. 15.

CHAPTER XVI

ere there arises a second question, when the Lord allows a wife to be put away for the cause of fornication, in what latitude of meaning fornication is to be understood in this passage,—whether in the sense understood by all, viz. that we are to understand that fornication to be meant which is committed in acts of uncleanness; or whether, in accordance with the usage of Scripture in speaking of fornication (as has been mentioned above), as meaning all unlawful corruption, such as idolatry or covetousness, and therefore, of course, every transgression of the law on account of the unlawful lust [involved in it].[140] But let us consult

---

140 Augustine expresses himself (*Retract.* I. xix. 6) as having misgivings about his own explanation of this matter here. He advises readers to go to his other writings on the subject of marriage and divorce, or to the works of other writers. He says all sin is not fornication (*omne peccatum fornicatio non est*); and to determine which sins are fornication, and when a wife may be dismissed, is a

the apostle, that we may not say rashly. "And unto the married I command," says he, "yet not I, but the Lord, Let not the wife depart from her husband: but and if she depart, let her remain unmarried, or be reconciled to her husband." For it may happen that she departs for that cause for which the Lord gives permission to do so. Or, if a woman is at liberty to put away her husband for other causes besides that of fornication, and the husband is not at liberty, what answer shall we give respecting this statement which he has made afterwards, "And let not the husband put away his wife"? Wherefore did he not add, saving for the cause of fornication, which the Lord permits, unless because he wishes a similar rule to be understood, that if he shall put away his wife (which he is permitted to do for the cause of fornication), he is to remain without a wife, or be reconciled to his wife? For it would not be a bad thing for a husband to be reconciled to such a woman as that to whom, when nobody had dared to

---

most broad (*latebrosissima*) question. He calls the question a most difficult (*difficillimam*) one, and says, "But verily I feel that I have not come to the perfect conclusion of this matter (*imo non me per-venisse ad hujus rei perfectionem sentio.*" *Retract.* ii. 57). Some of his treatises on the marriage relation: *De Bono Conjugali; De Conjugiis Adulterinis; De Nuptiis et Concupiscientia.*

stone her, the Lord said, "Go, and sin no more."[141] And
for this reason also, because He who says, It is not lawful to put away one's wife saving for the cause of fornication, forces him to retain his wife, if there should be
no cause of fornication: but if there should be, He does
not force him to put her away, but permits him, just
as when it is said, Let it not be lawful for a woman to
marry another, unless her husband be dead; if she shall
marry before the death of her husband, she is guilty;
if she shall not marry after the death of her husband,
she is not guilty, for she is not commanded to marry,
but merely permitted. If, therefore, there is a like rule
in the said law of marriage between man and woman,
to such an extent that not merely of the woman has
the same apostle said, "The wife hath not power of her
own body, but the husband;" but he has not been silent
respecting him, saying, "And likewise also the husband
hath not power of his own body, but the wife;"—if,
then, the rule is similar, there is no necessity for understanding that it is lawful for a woman to put away her
husband, saving for the cause of fornication, as is the
case also with the husband.

---

141 John viii. 11. *Vide deinceps ne pecces*; Vulgate, *jam amplius noli
peccare.*

It is therefore to be considered in what latitude of meaning we ought to understand the word fornication, and the apostle is to be consulted, as we were beginning to do. For he goes on to say, "But to the rest speak I, not the Lord." Here, first, we must see who are "the rest," for he was speaking before on the part of the Lord to those who are married, but now, as from himself, he speaks to "the rest:" hence perhaps to the unmarried, but this does not follow. For thus he continues: "If any brother hath a wife that believeth not, and she be pleased to dwell with him, let him not put her away." Hence, even now he is speaking to those who are married. What, then, is his object in saying "to the rest," unless that he was speaking before to those who were so united, that they were alike as to their faith in Christ; but that now he is speaking to "the rest," *i.e.* to those who are so united, that they are not both believers? But what does he say to them? "If any brother hath a wife that believeth not, and she be pleased to dwell with him, let him not put her away. And the woman which hath an husband that believeth not, and if he be pleased to dwell with her, let her not put him away." If, therefore, he does not give a command as from the Lord, but advises as from himself, then this good result springs from it, that if any one act otherwise, he is not a transgressor of a command, just as he says a little after respecting virgins, that he has no command of the Lord, but that he gives his advice; and he so praises virginity, that whoever will may avail himself of it; yet if he shall not do so, he may not be judged to have acted contrary to a command. For there is one thing which is commanded, another respecting which advice is given, another still which is allowed.[142] A wife is commanded not to depart from her husband; and if she depart, to remain unmarried, or to be reconciled to her husband: therefore it is not allowable for her to act otherwise. But a believing husband is advised, if he has an unbelieving wife who is pleased to dwell with him, not to put her away: therefore it is allowable also to put her away, because it is no command of the Lord that he should not put her away, but an advice of the apostle: just as a virgin is advised not to marry; but if she shall marry, she will not indeed adhere to the advice, but she will not act in opposition to a command. Allowance is given[143] when it is said, "But I speak this by permission, and not of commandment." And therefore, if it is allowable that an unbelieving wife should be put away, although it is better not to put her away, and yet not allowable, according to the commandment of the Lord, that a wife should

---

142 *Ignoscitur*, lit. "is pardoned."
143 Lit. "it is pardoned."

be put away, saving for the cause of fornication, [then] unbelief itself also is fornication.

For what sayest thou, O apostle? Surely, that a believing husband who has an unbelieving wife pleased to dwell with him is not to put her away? Just so, says he. When, therefore, the Lord also gives this command, that a man should not put away his wife, saving for the cause of fornication, why dost thou say here, "I speak, not the Lord"? For this reason, viz. that the idolatry which unbelievers follow, and every other noxious superstition, is fornication. Now, the Lord permitted a wife to be put away for the cause of fornication; but in permitting, He did not command it: He gave opportunity to the apostle for advising that whoever wished should not put away an unbelieving wife, in order that, perchance, in this way she might become a believer. "For," says he, "the unbelieving husband is sanctified in the wife, and the unbelieving wife is sanctified in the brother."[144] I suppose it had already occurred that some wives were embracing the faith by means of their believing husbands, and husbands by means of their believing wives; and although not mentioning names,

---

144 1 Cor. vii. 14. Augustine conforms to the approved reading in the Greek text: *in uxore…in fratre*. Vulgate, *per mulierem,…per virum*. (See Revised Version.)

he yet urged his case by examples, in order to strengthen his counsel. Then he goes on to say, "Else were your children unclean; but now are they holy." For now the children were Christians, who were sanctified at the instance of one of the parents, or with the consent of both; which would not take place unless the marriage were broken up by one of the parties becoming a believer, and unless the unbelief of the spouse were borne with so far as to give an opportunity of believing. This, therefore, is the counsel of Him whom I regard as having spoken the words, "Whatsoever thou spendest more, when I come again, I will repay thee."[145]

Moreover, if unbelief is fornication, and idolatry unbelief, and covetousness idolatry, it is not to be doubted that covetousness also is fornication. Who, then, in that case can rightly separate any unlawful lust whatever from the category of fornication, if covetousness is fornication? And from this we perceive, that because of unlawful lusts, not only those of which one is guilty in acts of uncleanness with another's husband or wife, but any unlawful lusts whatever, which cause the soul making a bad use of the body to wander from the law of God, and to be ruinously and basely corrupted,

---

145 Luke x. 35.

a man may, without crime, put away his wife, and a wife her husband, because the Lord makes the cause of fornication an exception; which fornication, in accordance with the above considerations, we are compelled to understand as being general and universal.

But when He says, "saving for the cause of fornication," He has not said of which of them, whether the man or the woman.[146] For not only is it allowed to put away a wife who commits fornication; but whoever puts away that wife even by whom he is himself compelled to commit fornication, puts her away undoubtedly for the cause of fornication. As, for instance, if a wife should compel one to sacrifice to idols, the man who puts away such an one puts her away for the cause of fornication, not only on her part, but on his own also: on her part, because she commits fornication; on his own, that he may not commit fornication. Nothing, however, is more unjust than for a man to put away his wife because of

---

146 Modern commentators do not spring this question, agreeing that the fornication referred to is of the wife. Paulus, Döllinger (in *Christ. u. Kirche*, to which Professor Conington replied in *Cont. Rev.*, May, 1869) think the fornication of the woman was committed before her marriage. Plumptre also prefers the reference to antenuptial sin.

fornication, if he himself also is convicted of committing fornication. For that passage occurs to one: "For wherein thou judgest another, thou condemnest thyself; for thou that judgest doest the same things."[147] And for this reason, whosoever wishes to put away his wife because of fornication, ought first to be cleared of fornication; and a like remark I would make respecting the woman also.

But in reference to what He says, "Whosoever shall marry her that is divorced[148] committeth adultery," it may be asked whether she also who is married commits adultery in the same way as he does who marries her. For she also is commanded to remain unmarried, or be reconciled to her husband; but this in the case of her departing from her husband. There is, however, a great difference whether she put away or be put away. For if she put away her husband, and marry another, she seems to have left her former husband from a desire of changing her marriage connection, which is, without

---

147 Rom. ii. 1.

148 ‡ἀολελυμένην; that is, one divorced unlawfully who has not been guilty of fornication (so Meyer very positively, Stier *et. al.*, Alford hesitatingly). This explanation might seem to limit remarriage to such an one, inasmuch as the essence of the marriage bond has not been touched (So Alford *et. al.*).

doubt, an adulterous thought. But if she be put away by the husband, with whom she desired to be, he indeed who marries her commits adultery, according to the Lord's declaration; but whether she also be involved in a like crime is uncertain,—although it is much less easy to discover how, when a man and woman have intercourse one with another with equal consent, one of them should be an adulterer, and the other not. To this is to be added the consideration, that if he commits adultery by marrying her who is divorced from her husband (although she does not put away, but is put away), she causes him to commit adultery, which nevertheless the Lord forbids. And hence we infer that, whether she has been put away, or has put away her husband, it is necessary for her to remain unmarried, or be reconciled to her husband.[149]

Again, it is asked whether, if, with a wife's permission, either a barren one, or one who does not wish to submit to intercourse, a man shall take to himself another woman, not another man's wife, nor one separated from her husband, he can do so without being

---

[149] That is, innocent or guilty, she cannot marry without committing adultery. The Roman Catholic Church forbids divorces, but permits an indefinite separation *a mensa et toro* ("from table and bed").

chargeable with fornication? And an example is found in the Old Testament history;[150] but now there are greater precepts which the human race has reached after having passed that stage; and those matters are to be investigated for the purpose of distinguishing the ages of the dispensation of that divine providence which assists the human race in the most orderly way; but not for the purpose of making use of the rules of living. But yet it may be asked whether what the apostle says, "The wife hath not power of her own body, but the husband; and likewise also the husband hath not power of his own body, but the wife," can be carried so far, that, with the permission of a wife, who possesses the power over her husband's body, a man can have intercourse with another woman, who is neither another man's wife nor divorced from her husband; but such an opinion is not to be entertained, lest it should seem that a woman also, with her husband's permission, could do such a thing, which the instinctive feeling of every one prevents.

And yet some occasions may arise, where a wife also, with the consent of her husband, may seem under obligation to do this for the sake of that husband

---

150 Abraham taking Hagar with Sarah's consent.

himself; as, for instance, is said to have happened at Antioch about fifty years ago,[151] in the times of Constantius. For Acyndinus, at that time prefect and at one time also consul, when he demanded of a certain public debtor the payment of a poundweight of gold, impelled by I know not what motive, did a thing which is often dangerous in the case of those magistrates to whom anything whatever is lawful, or rather is thought to be lawful, viz. threatened with an oath and with a vehement affirmation, that if he did not pay the foresaid gold on a certain day which he had fixed, he would be put to death. Accordingly, while he was being kept in cruel confinement, and was unable to rid himself of that debt, the dread day began to impend and to draw near. He happened, however, to have a very beautiful wife, but one who had no money wherewith to come to the relief of her husband; and when a certain rich man had had his desires inflamed by the beauty of this woman, and had learned that her husband was placed in that critical situation, he sent to her, promising in return for a single night, if she would consent to hold intercourse with him, that he would give her the pound of gold. Then she, knowing that she herself had not

---

151 About the year 343; for Augustine wrote this treatise about the year 393.

power over her body, but her husband, conveyed the intelligence to him, telling him that she was prepared to do it for the sake of her husband, but only if he himself, the lord by marriage of her body, to whom all that chastity was due, should wish it to be done, as if disposing of his own property for the sake of his life. He thanked her, and commanded that it should be done, in no wise judging that it was an adulterous embrace, because it was no lust, but great love for her husband, that demanded it, at his own bidding and will. The woman came to the villa of that rich man, did what the lewd man wished; but she gave her body only to her husband, who desired not, as was usual, his marriage rights, but life. She received the gold; but he who gave it took away stealthily what he had given, and substituted a similar bag with earth in it. When the woman, however, on reaching her home, discovered it, she rushed forth in public in order to proclaim the deed she had done, animated by the same tender affection for her husband by which she had been forced to do it; she goes to the prefect, confesses everything, shows the fraud that had been practised upon her. Then indeed the prefect first pronounces himself guilty, because the matter had come to this by means of his threats, and, as if pronouncing sentence upon another, decided that a pound of gold should be brought into the treasury from the property of Acyndinus; but that she (the woman) be installed as mistress of that piece of land whence she had received the earth instead of the gold. I offer no opinion either way from this story: let each one form a judgment as he pleases, for the history is not drawn from divinely authoritative sources; but yet, when the story is related, man's instinctive sense does not so revolt against what was done in the case of this woman, at her husband's bidding, as we formerly shuddered when the thing itself was set forth without any example. But in this section of the Gospel nothing is to be more steadily kept in view, than that so great is the evil of fornication, that, while married people are bound to one another by so strong a bond, this one cause of divorce is excepted; but as to what fornication is, that we have already discussed.[152]

---

152 The law permitted divorce for "some uncleanness" (Deut. xxiv. 1). In the time of Christ divorce was allowed on trivial grounds. While Schammai interpreted the Deuteronomic prescription of *moral* uncleanness or adultery, Hillel interpreted it to include *physical* uncleanness or unattractiveness. A wife's cooking her husband's food unpalatably he declared to be a legitimate cause for dissolution of the marriage bond. Opposing the loose views current, Christ declared that it was on account of the "hardness of their hearts" that Moses had *suffered* them to put away their

wives, and asserted adultery to be the only allowable reason for divorce. The question whether the innocent party may marry, is beset with great difficulties in view of this passage and Matt. xix. 9. The answer turns somewhat upon the construction of the passage. Augustine here, the Council of Trent (and so the Roman Catholic Church), Weiss, Mansel, and others hold that all marriage of a divorced person is declared illegal. In another place (*De Conj. Adult.* i. 9) Augustine says, "Why, I say, did the Lord interject 'the cause of fornication,' and not say rather, in a general way, 'Whosoever shall put away his wife and marry another commits adultery'?...I think, because the Lord wishes to mention that which is greater. For who will deny that it is a greater adultery to marry another when the divorced wife has not committed fornication than when any one divorces his wife and then marries another? Not because this is not adultery, but because it is a lesser sort." The *Apost. Constitutions* (vii. 2) say, "Thou shalt not commit adultery, for thou dividest one flesh into two," etc. Weiss: "Jesus everywhere takes it for granted that in the sight of God there is no such thing as a dissolution of the marriage bond" (*Leben Jesu*, i. 529). President Woolsey, on the other hand, unhesitatingly declares, that, by Christ's precepts, marriage is dissolved by adultery, so that the innocent party may marry again. According to this passage, the woman divorced on other grounds than adultery seems to be declared adulterous if she marry. According to Matt. xix. 9 the man who puts away his wife for adultery, seems to be permitted to marry without becoming adulterous himself. According to Mark x. 12 the woman had the privilege in that day of putting away her husband, but "there is no evidence in the Hebrew Scriptures that the woman could get herself divorced from her husband." To the able treatment of Augustine, which might seem either exceedingly

fearless or mawkish at the present day, according to the standpoint
of the critic, the reader would do well to read Alford and Lange on
this passage; Stanley on 1 Cor. vii. 11; and Woolsey, art. "Divorce"
in *Schaff-Herzog Encycl*. Whatever may be the exact meaning of
our Lord concerning the marriage of the innocent party, it is evident that He regards the marriage bond as profoundly sacred,
and warrants the celebrant in binding the parties to marriage to
be faithful one to the other "till death do you part." He Himself
said, "What, therefore, God hath joined together, let not man put
asunder" (Mark x. 9).

CHAPTER XVII

"Again," says He, "ye have heard that it hath been said to them of old time, Thou shalt not forswear thyself, but shalt perform unto the Lord thine oath:[153] But I say unto you, Swear not at all; neither by heaven, for it is God's throne; nor by the earth, for it is His footstool; neither by Jerusalem, for it is the city of the great King. Neither shalt thou swear by thy head, because thou canst not make one hair white or black. But let your communication be Yea, yea; Nay, nay: for whatsoever is more[154] than these cometh of evil." The righteousness of the Pharisees is not to forswear oneself; and this is confirmed by Him who gives the command not to swear, so far as relates to the righteousness of the kingdom of heaven. For just as he who does not speak at all cannot speak falsely, so he who does not swear

---

[153] *Jusjurandum*; Vulgate, *juramenta*; Greek, τοὺς ὅρκους.

[154] *Amplius*; Vulgate, *abundantius*.

at all cannot swear falsely. But yet, since he who takes God to witness swears, this section must be carefully considered, lest the apostle should seem to have acted contrary to the Lord's precept, who often swore in this way, when he says, "Now the things which I write unto you, behold, before God I lie not;"[155] and again, "The God and Father of our Lord Jesus Christ, which is blessed for evermore, knoweth that I lie not."[156] Of like nature also is that asseveration, "For God is my witness, whom I serve with my spirit in the gospel of His Son, that without ceasing I make mention of you always in my prayers."[157] Unless, perchance, one were to say that it is to be reckoned swearing only when something is spoken of by which one swears; so that he has not used an oath, because he has not said, by God; but has said, "God is witness." It is ridiculous to think so; yet because of the contentious, or those very slow of apprehension, lest any one should think there is a difference, let him know that the apostle has used an oath in this way also, saying, "By your rejoicing, I die daily."[158] And let no one think that this is so expressed as if it were said, Your

---

155 Gal. i. 20.

156 2 Cor. xi. 31.

157 Rom. i. 9.

158 1 Cor. xv. 31.

rejoicing makes me die daily; just as it is said, By his teaching he became learned, *i.e.* by his teaching it came about that he was perfectly instructed: the Greek copies decide the matter, where we find it written, Νὴ τὴν καύχησιν ὑμετέραν, an expression which is used only by one taking an oath. Thus, then, it is understood that the Lord gave the command not to swear in this sense, lest any one should eagerly seek after an oath as a good thing, and by the constant use of oaths sink down through force of habit into perjury. And therefore let him who understands that swearing is to be reckoned not among things that are good, but among things that are necessary, refrain as far as he can from indulging in it, unless by necessity, when he sees men slow to believe what it is useful for them to believe, except they be assured by an oath. To this, accordingly, reference is made when it is said, "Let your speech be, Yea, yea; Nay, nay;" this is good, and what is to be desired. "For whatsoever is more than these cometh of evil;" *i.e.*, if you are compelled to swear, know that it comes of a necessity arising from the infirmity of those whom you are trying to persuade of something; which infirmity is certainly an evil, from which we daily pray to be delivered, when we say, "Deliver us from evil."[159] Hence He has not said, Whatsoever is more than these is evil; for you are not doing what is evil when you make a good use of an oath, which, although not in itself good, is yet necessary in order to persuade another that you are trying to move him for some useful end; but it "cometh of evil" on his part by whose infirmity you are compelled to swear.[160] But no one learns, unless he has had experience, how difficult it is both to get rid of a habit of swearing, and never to do rashly what necessity sometimes compels him to do.[161]

---

159 Matt. vi. 13.

160 Revised Version, *Evil One*. So Euthymius, Zig. (*auctorem habet diabolum*), Chrysostom, Theophylact, Fritzsche, Keim, Meyer, Plumptre, etc. The interpretation of Augustine is shared by Luther, Bengel, De Wette, Tholuck, Ewald, etc.

161 Augustine is somewhat perplexed about the meaning, but decides the injunction to be directed against the abuse of the oath, not to forbid it wholly. The oath was permitted by the law (Lev. xxii. 11), was to be held sacred (Num. xxx. 2), and to be made in God's name (Deut. vi. 13). It was customary under the Old Testament to swear (Gen. xxiv. 37, Josh. ix. 15; perhaps only a solemn affirmation), and in the name of the Lord (1 Sam. xx. 42; Irenæus, Clement, Origen, Chrysostom, etc.). The Anabaptists, Mennonites, and Quakers understand the precept to forbid all oaths, even in the civil court. "Christendom, if it were fully conformed to Christ's will, as it should be, would tolerate no

oaths whatever" (Meyer). "The proper state of Christians is to require no oaths" (Alford). If interpreted as a definite prohibition
of all swearing, the passage comes into conflict with Christ's own
example (Matt. xxvi. 63), and the apostle's conduct in the passages quoted by Augustine. The meaning has been restricted to
rash and frivolous oaths on the street and in the market (Keim);
in daily conversation (Carr, *Camb. Bible for Schools*). In the ideal Christian community, where truth and honesty prevail, oaths
will be superfluous: the simple asseverations, "Yea, nay," will be
sufficient. To this, Christ's precept ultimately looks. But He, no
doubt, had in mind the widespread profanity of His day, and the
current opinion that only oaths containing the name of God were
binding (Lightfoot cites from the Rabbinical books to this effect).
All unnecessary appeals to God, as well as careless and profane
swearing, are forbidden, as coming either from bad passions within or a want of reverence. "Prohibition would be repeal of the
Mosaic law" (Plumptre). "All strengthening of the simple 'Yea and
nay' is occasioned by the presence of sin and Satan in the world.
There is no more striking proof of the existence of evil than the
prevalence of the foolish, low, useless habit of swearing. It could
never have arisen if men did not believe each other to be liars,"
etc. (Schaff). "Men use their protestations because they are distrustful one of another. An oath is physic, which supposes disease"
(M. Henry). When the oath is performed for the "sake of ethical
interests, as when the civil authority demands it," as seems to be
necessary and safe for society in its present unsanctified condition,
the precept does not interfere (Köstlin, art. "Oath," *Schaff-Herzog
Encycl.*, Meyer, Wuttke, Alford, Tholuck, etc.). An interesting imitation of the Rabbinical casuistry above referred to was practised
by the crafty and subtle Louis XI. Scott says (Introd. to *Quentin*

But it may be asked why, when it was said, "But I say unto you, Swear not at all," it was added, "neither by heaven, for it is God's throne," etc., up to "neither by thy head." I suppose it was for this reason, that the Jews did not think they were bound by the oath, if they had sworn by such things: and since they had heard it said, "Thou shalt perform unto the Lord thine oath," they did not think an oath brought them under obligation to the Lord, if they swore by heaven, or earth, or by Jerusalem, or by their head; and this happened not from the fault of Him who gave the command, but because they did not rightly understand it. Hence the Lord teaches that there is nothing so worthless among the creatures of God, as that any one should think that he may swear falsely by it; since created things, from the highest down to the lowest, beginning with the throne of God and going down to a white or black hair, are ruled by divine providence. "Neither by heaven," says He, "for it is God's throne; nor by the earth, for it is His footstool:" *i.e.*, when you swear by heaven or the earth, do not imagine that your oath does not bring

---

Durward), "He admitted to one or two peculiar forms of oath the force of a binding obligation which he denied to all others, strictly preserving the secret; which mode of swearing he really accounted obligatory, as one of the most valuable of State secrets."

you under obligation to the Lord; for you are convicted of swearing by Him who has heaven for His throne, and the earth for His footstool. "Neither by Jerusalem, for it is the city of the great King;" a better expression than if He had said, "My [city];" although, however, we understand Him to have meant this. And, because He is undoubtedly the Lord, the man who swears by Jerusalem is bound by his oath to the Lord. "Neither shall thou swear by thy head." Now, what could any one suppose to belong more to himself than his own head? But how is it ours, when we have not the power of making one hair white or black? Hence, whoever should wish to swear even by his own head, is bound by his oath to God, who in an ineffable way keeps all things in His power, and is everywhere present. And here also all other things are understood, which could not of course be enumerated; just as that saying of the apostle we have mentioned, "By your rejoicing, I die daily." And to show that he was bound by this oath to the Lord, he has added, "which I have in Christ Jesus."

But yet (I make the remark for the sake of the carnal) we must not think that heaven is called God's throne, and the earth His footstool, because God has members placed in heaven and in earth, in some such way as we have when we sit down; but that seat means judgment. And since, in this organic whole of the universe, heaven has the greatest appearance, and earth the least,—as if the divine power were more present where the beauty excels, but still were regulating the least degree of it in the most distant and in the lowest regions,—He is said to sit in heaven, and to tread upon the earth. But spiritually the expression heaven means holy souls, and earth sinful ones: and since the spiritual man judges all things, yet he himself is judged of no man,[162] he is suitably spoken of as the seat of God; but the sinner to whom it is said, "Earth thou art, and unto earth shall thou return,"[163] because, in accordance with that justice which assigns what is suitable to men's deserts, he is placed among things that are lowest, and he who would not remain in the law is punished under the law, is suitably taken as His footstool.

---

162 1 Cor. ii. 15.
163 Gen. iii. 19.

CHAPTER XVIII

B ut now, to conclude by summing up this passage, what can be named or thought of more laborious and toilsome, where the believing soul is straining every nerve of its industry, than the subduing of vicious habit? Let such an one cut off the members which obstruct the kingdom of heaven, and not be overwhelmed by the pain: in conjugal fidelity let him bear with everything which, however grievously annoying it may be, is still free from the guilt of unlawful corruption, *i.e.* of fornication: as, for instance, if any one should have a wife either barren, or misshapen in body, or faulty in her members,—either blind, or deaf, or lame, or having any other defect,—or worn out by diseases and pains and weaknesses, and whatever else may be thought of exceeding horrible, fornication excepted, let him endure it for the sake of his plighted

love and conjugal union;[164] and let him not only not
put away such a wife, but even if he have her not, let
him not marry one who has been divorced by her husband, though beautiful, healthy, rich, fruitful. And if
it is not lawful to do such things, much less is it to be
deemed lawful for him to come near any other unlawful embrace; and let him so flee from fornication, as to
withdraw himself from base corruption of every sort.
Let him speak the truth, and let him commend it not
by frequent oaths, but by the probity of his morals;
and with respect to the innumerable crowds of all bad
habits rising up in rebellion against him, of which,
in order that all may be understood, a few have been
mentioned, let him betake himself to the citadel of
Christian warfare, and let him lay them prostrate, as if
from a higher ground. But who would venture to enter
upon labours so great, unless one who is so inflamed
with the love of righteousness, that, as it were utterly
consumed with hunger and thirst, and thinking there
is no life for him till that is satisfied, he puts forth violence to obtain the kingdom of heaven? For otherwise
he will not be able bravely to endure all those things
which the lovers of this world reckon toilsome and

---

164 *Pro fide et societate.*

arduous, and altogether difficult in getting rid of bad habits. "Blessed," therefore, "are they which do hunger and thirst after righteousness: for they shall be filled."

But yet, when any one encounters difficulty in these toils, and advancing through hardships and roughnesses surrounded with various temptations, and perceiving the troubles of his past life rise up on this side and on that, becomes afraid lest he should not be able to carry through what he has undertaken, let him eagerly avail himself of the counsel that he may obtain assistance. But what other counsel is there than this, that he who desires to have divine help for his own infirmity should bear that of others, and should assist it as much as possible? And so, therefore, let us look at the precepts of mercy. The meek and the merciful man, however, seem to be one and the same: but there is this difference, that the meek man, of whom we have spoken above, from piety does not gainsay the divine sentences which are brought forward against his sins, nor those statements of God which he does not yet understand; but he confers no benefit on him whom he does not gainsay or resist. But the merciful man in such a way offers no resistance, that he does it for the purpose of correcting him whom he would render worse by resisting.

Chapter XIX

Hence the Lord goes on to say: "Ye have heard that it hath been said, An eye for an eye, and a tooth for a tooth: but I say unto you, that ye resist not evil;[165] but whosoever shall smite thee on thy right cheek, turn to him the other also. And if any man will sue thee at the law, and take away thy coat [tunic, undergarment], let him have thy cloak[166] also. And whosoever shall compel thee to go a mile, go with him twain. Give to him that asketh thee,[167] and from him that would borrow of thee turn not thou away." It is the lesser righteousness of the Pharisees not to go beyond measure in revenge, that no one should give back more than he has received: and this is a great step. For it is not easy to find any one who, when he has received a blow, wishes

---

165 *Adversus malum*; Vulgate, *malo*.

166 *Vestimentum*; Vulgate, *pallium*.

167 *Omni petenti te, da*; Vulgate, *qui petit a te*, etc.

merely to return the blow; and who, on hearing one word from a man who reviles him, is content to return only one, and that just an equivalent; but he avenges it more immoderately, either under the disturbing influence of anger, or because he thinks it just, that he who first inflicted injury should suffer more severe injury than he suffered who had not inflicted injury. Such a spirit was in great measure restrained by the law, where it was written, "An eye for an eye, and a tooth for a tooth;" by which expressions a certain measure is intended, so that the vengeance should not exceed the injury. And this is the beginning of peace: but perfect peace is to have no wish at all for such vengeance.

Hence, between that first course which goes beyond the law, that a greater evil should be inflicted in return for a lesser, and this to which the Lord has given expression for the purpose of perfecting the disciples, that no evil at all should be inflicted in return for evil, a middle course holds a certain place, viz. that as much be paid back as has been received; by means of which enactment the transition is made from the highest discord to the highest concord, according to the distribution of times. See, therefore, at how great a distance any one who is the first to do harm to another, with the desire of injuring and hurting him, stands from him who, even when injured, does not pay back the injury. That man, however, who is not the first to do harm to any one, but who yet, when injured, inflicts a greater injury in return, either in will or in deed, has so far withdrawn himself from the highest injustice, and made so far an advance to the highest righteousness; but still he does not yet hold by what the law given by Moses commanded. And therefore he who pays back just as much as he has received already forgives something: for the party who injures does not deserve merely as much punishment as the man who was injured by him has innocently suffered. And accordingly this incomplete, by no means severe, but [rather] merciful justice, is carried to perfection by Him who came to fulfil the law, not to destroy it. Hence there are still two intervening steps which He has left to be understood, while He has chosen rather to speak of the very highest development of mercy. For there is still what one may do who does not come fully up to that magnitude of the precept which belongs to the kingdom of heaven; acting in such a way that he does not pay back as much, but less; as, for instance, one blow instead of two, or that he cuts off an ear for an eye that has been plucked out. He who, rising above this, pays back nothing at all, approaches the Lord's precept, but yet he does not reach it. For still it seems to the Lord not enough, if, for the evil which you may have received, you should inflict no evil in return, unless you be prepared to receive even more. And therefore He does not say, "But I say unto you," that you are not to return evil for evil; although even this would be a great precept: but He says, "that ye resist not evil;"[168] so that not only are you not to pay back what may have been inflicted on you, but you are not even to resist other inflictions. For this is what He also goes on to explain: "But whosoever shall smite thee on thy right cheek, turn to him the other also:" for He does not say, If any man smite thee, do not wish to smite him; but, Offer thyself further to him if he should go on to smite thee. As regards compassion, they feel it most who minister to those whom they greatly love as if they were their children, or some very dear friends in sickness, or little children, or insane persons, at whose hands they often endure

---

168 With Augustine, Calvin, Tholuck, Ewald, Lange construe this as neuter, *evil*; Chrysostom, Theophylact, *the devil*; De Wette, Meyer, Alford, Plumptre, as also the Revised Version, *the man who does evil*. Renan says the practice of this doctrine put down slavery: "It was not Spartacus who suppressed slavery, but rather was it Blandina" ("*Ce n'est pas Spartacus qui a supprimé l'esclavage, c'est bien plûtôt Blandine*").

many things; and if their welfare demand it, they even show themselves ready to endure more, until the weakness either of age or of disease pass away. And so, as regards those whom the Lord, the Physician of souls, was instructing to take care of their neighbours, what else could He teach them, than that they endure quietly the infirmities of those whose welfare they wish to consult? For all wickedness arises from infirmity[169] of mind: because nothing is more harmless than the man who is perfect in virtue.

But it may be asked what the right cheek means. For this is the reading we find in the Greek copies, which are most worthy of confidence; though many Latin ones have only the word "cheek," without the addition of "right." Now the face is that by which any one is recognised; and we read in the apostle's writings, "For ye suffer,[170] if a man bring you into bondage, if a man devour you, if a man take of you, if a man exalt himself, if a man smite you on the face:" then immediately he adds, "I speak as concerning reproach;"[171] so that he explains what striking on the face is, viz. to be contemned and despised. Nor is this indeed said by the

---

169 *Imbecillitate.*

170 *Toleratis*; Vulgate, *sustinetis.*

171 2 Cor. xi. 20, 21.

apostle for this reason, that they should not bear with those parties; but that they should bear with himself rather, who so loved them, that he was willing that he himself should be spent for them.[172] But since the face cannot be called right and left, and yet there may be a worth according to the estimate of God and according to the estimate of this world, it is so distributed as it were into the right and left cheek that whatever disciple of Christ might have to bear reproach for being a Christian, he should be much more ready to bear reproach in himself, if he possesses any of the honours of this world. Thus this same apostle, if he had kept silence respecting the dignity which he had in the world, when men were persecuting in him the Christian name, would not have presented the other cheek to those that were smiting the right one. For when he said, I am a Roman citizen,[173] he was not unprepared to submit to be despised, in that which he reckoned as least, by those who had despised in him so precious and life-giving a name. For did he at all the less on that account afterwards submit to the chains, which it was not lawful to put on Roman citizens, or did he wish to accuse any one of this injury? And if any spared him

172 2 Cor. xii. 15.
173 Acts xxii. 25.

on account of the name of Roman citizenship, yet he did not on that account refrain from offering an object they might strike at, since he wished by his patience to cure of so great perversity those whom he saw honouring in him what belonged to the left members rather than the right. For that point only is to be attended to, in what spirit he did everything, how benevolently and mildly he acted toward those from whom he was suffering such things. For when he was smitten with the hand by order of the high priest, what he seemed to say contumeliously when he affirms, "God shall smite thee, thou whited wall," sounds like an insult to those who do not understand it; but to those who do, it is a prophecy. For a whited wall is hypocrisy, *i.e.* pretence holding forth the sacerdotal dignity before itself, and under this name, as under a white covering, concealing an inner and as it were sordid baseness. For what belonged to humility he wonderfully preserved, when, on its being said to him, "Revilest thou the high priest?"[174] he replied, "I wist not, brethren, that he was the high priest; for it is written, Thou shall not speak evil of the ruler of thy people."[175] And here he showed with what calmness he had spoken that which he seemed to have

---

174 *Principi sacerdotum*; Vulgate, *summum sacerdotem*.
175 Acts xxiii. 3-5.

spoken in anger, because he answered so quickly and
so mildly, which cannot be done by those who are in-
dignant and thrown into confusion. And in that very
statement he spoke the truth to those who understood
him, "I wist not that he was the high priest:"[176] as if
he said, I know another High Priest, for whose name
I bear such things, whom it is not lawful to revile, and
whom ye revile, since in me it is nothing else but His
name that ye hate. Thus, therefore, it is necessary for
one not to boast of such things in a hypocritical way,
but to be prepared in the heart itself for all things, so
that he can sing that prophetic word, "My heart is prepared,[177] O God, my heart is prepared." For many have
learned how to offer the other cheek, but do not know
how to love him by whom they are struck. But in truth,
the Lord Himself, who certainly was the first to fulfil
the precepts which He taught, did not offer the other
cheek to the servant of the high priest when smiting
Him thereon; but, so far from that, said, "If I have spoken evil, hear witness of the evil;[178] but if well, why

---

176 Interpreted by modern commentators usually of temporary
forgetfulness, or, what is much better, failure to recognise through
infirmity of vision.

177 English version, "fixed"— Ps. lvii. 7.

178 *Exprobra de malo*; Vulgate, *testimonium perhibe de malo*.

smitest thou me?"[179] Yet was He not on that account unprepared in heart, for the salvation of all, not merely to be smitten on the other cheek, but even to have His whole body crucified.

Hence also what follows, "And if any man will sue thee at the law, and take away thy coat, let him have thy cloak[180] also," is rightly understood as a precept having reference to the preparation of heart, not to a vain show of outward deed. But what is said with respect to the coat and cloak is to be carried out not merely in such things, but in the case of everything which on any ground of right we speak of as being ours for time. For if this command is given with respect to what is necessary, how much more does it become us to contemn what is superfluous! But still, those things which I have called ours are to be included in that category under which the Lord Himself gives the precept, when He says, "If any man will sue thee at the law, and take away thy coat." Let all these things therefore be understood for which we may be sued at the law, so that the right to them may pass from us to him who sues, or for whom he sues; such, for instance, as clothing, a house,

179 John xviii. 23.
180 The coat or tunic was the *undergarment*. The cloak, or pallium, was the *outergarment*, and the more precious.

an estate, a beast of burden, and in general all kinds of property. But whether it is to be understood of slaves also is a great question. For a Christian ought not to possess a slave in the same way as a horse or money: although it may happen that a horse is valued at a greater price than a slave, and some article of gold or silver at much more. But with respect to that slave, if he is being educated and ruled by time as his master, in a way more upright, and more honourable, and more conducing to the fear of God, than can be done by him who desires to take him away, I do not know whether any one would dare to say that he ought to be despised like a garment. For a man ought to love a fellow man as himself, inasmuch as he is commanded by the Lord of all (as is shown by what follows) even to love his enemies.

It is carefully to be observed that every tunic[181] is a garment,[182] but that every garment is not a tunic. Hence the word garment means more than the word tunic. And therefore I think it is so expressed, "And if any one will sue thee at the law, and take away thy tunic, let him have thy garment also," as if He had said, Whoever wishes to take away thy tunic, give over to him whatever other clothing thou hast. And so some

---

181 English version, "coat."
182 English version, "cloak."

have interpreted the word *pallium*, which in the Greek as used here is ἱμάτιον.

"And whosoever," says He, "shall compel[183] thee to go a mile, go with him other two." And this, certainly, not so much in the sense that thou shouldest do it on foot, as that thou shouldest be prepared in mind to do it. For in the Christian history itself, which is authoritative, you will find no such thing done by the saints, or by the Lord Himself when in His human nature, which He condescended to assume, He was showing us an example of how to live; while at the same time, in almost all places, you will find them prepared to bear with equanimity whatever may have been wickedly forced upon them. But are we to suppose it is said for the sake of the mere expression, "Go with him other two;" or did He rather wish that three should be completed,—the number which has the meaning of perfection; so that every one should remember when he does this, that he is fulfilling perfect righteousness by compassionately bearing the infirmities of those whom he wishes to be made whole? It may seem for this reason also that He has recommended these precepts by

---

183 The Greek word ἀγγαρεύω is derived from the Persian, to press one into service, as a courier to bear despatches. (See Thayer, *Lexicon*.)

three examples: of which the first is, if any one shall smite thee on the cheek; the second, if any one shall wish to take away thy coat; the third, if any one shall compel thee to go a mile: in which third example twice as much is added to the original unit, so that in this way the triplet is completed. And if this number in the passage before us does not, as has been said, mean perfection, let this be understood, that in laying down His precepts, as it were beginning with what is more tolerable, He has gradually gone on, until He has reached as far as the enduring of twice as much more. For, in the first place, He wished the other cheek to be presented when the right had been smitten, so that you may be prepared to bear less than you have borne. For whatever the right means, it is at least something more dear than that which is meant by the left; and if one who has borne with something in what is more dear, bears with it in what is less dear, it is something less. Then, secondly, in the case of one who wishes to take away a coat, He enjoins that the garment also should be given up to him: which is either just as much, or not much more; not, however, twice as much. In the third place, with respect to the mile, to which He says that two miles are to be added, He enjoins that you should bear with even twice as much more: thus signifying that whether it be somewhat less than the original demand, or just as much, or more, that any wicked man shall wish to take from thee, it is to be borne with tranquil mind.

Chapter XX

A nd, indeed, in these three classes of examples, I
see that no class of injury is passed over.[184] For
all matters in which we suffer any injustice are divided
into two classes: of which the one is, where restitution
cannot be made; the other, where it can. But in that
case where restitution cannot be made, a compensation
in revenge is usually sought. For what does it profit,
that on being struck you strike in return? Is that part
of the body which was injured for that reason restored
to its original condition? But an excited mind desires
such alleviations. Things of that sort, however, afford
no pleasure to a healthy and firm one; nay, such an one
judges rather that the other's infirmity is to be compassionately borne with, than that his own (which has
no existence) should be soothed by the punishment of
another.

---

184 *Exemplum citatur injuriæ privatæ, forensis, curialis* (Bengel).

Nor are we thus precluded from inflicting such punishment [requital][185] as avails for correction, and as compassion itself dictates; nor does it stand in the way of that course proposed, where one is prepared to endure more at the hand of him whom he wishes to set right. But no one is fit for inflicting this punishment except the man who, by the greatness of his love, has overcome that hatred wherewith those are wont to be inflamed who wish to avenge themselves. For it is not to be feared that parents would seem to hate a little son when, on committing an offence, he is beaten by them that he may not go on offending. And certainly the perfection of love is set before us by the imitation of God the Father Himself when it is said in what follows: "Love your enemies, do good to them that hate you, and pray for them[186] which persecute you;" and yet it is said of Him by the prophet, "For whom the Lord loveth He correcteth; yea, He scourgeth every son whom He receiveth."[187] The Lord also says, "The servant that knows not[188] his Lord's will, and does things

---

185 *Vindicta.*

186 *Pro eis qui vos persequuntur;* Vulgate, *pro persequentibus.*

187 Prov. iii. 12. So the LXX. English version: "even as a father the son in whom he delighteth," following the Hebrew.

188 *Nescit;* Vulgate, *non cognovit.*

worthy of stripes, shall be beaten with few stripes; but the servant that knows his Lord's will, and does things worthy of stripes, shall be beaten with many stripes."[189] No more, therefore, is sought for, except that he should punish to whom, in the natural order of things, the power is given; and that he should punish with the same goodwill which a father has towards his little son, whom by reason of his youth he cannot yet hate. For from this source the most suitable example is drawn, in order that it may be sufficiently manifest that sin can be punished in love rather than be left unpunished; so that one may wish him on whom he inflicts it not to be miserable by means of punishment, but to be happy by means of correction, yet be prepared, if need be, to endure with equanimity more injuries inflicted by him whom he wishes to be corrected, whether he may have the power of putting restraint upon him or not.

But great and holy men, although they at the time knew excellently well that that death which separates the soul from the body is not to be dreaded, yet, in accordance with the sentiment of those who might fear it, punished some sins with death, both because the living were struck with a salutary fear, and because it

---

189 Luke xii. 48, 47.

was not death itself that would injure those who were being punished with death, but sin, which might be increased if they continued to live. They did not judge rashly on whom God had bestowed such a power of judging. Hence it is that Elijah inflicted death on many, both with his own hand[190] and by calling down fire from heaven;[191] as was done also without rashness by many other great and godlike men, in the same spirit of concern for the good of humanity. And when the disciples had quoted an example from this Elias, mentioning to the Lord what had been done by him, in order that He might give to themselves also the power of calling down fire from heaven to consume those who would not show Him hospitality, the Lord reproved in them, not the example of the holy prophet, but their ignorance in respect to taking vengeance, their knowledge being as yet elementary;[192] perceiving that they did not in love desire correction, but in hated desired revenge. Accordingly, after He had taught them what it was to love one's neighbour as oneself, and when the Holy Spirit had been poured out, whom, at the end of ten days after His ascension, He sent from above, as

---

190 1 Kings xviii. 40.

191 2 Kings i. 10.

192 Luke ix. 52-56.

He had promised,[193] there were not wanting such acts of vengeance, although much more rarely than in the Old Testament. For there, for the most part, as servants they were kept down by fear; but here mostly as free they were nourished by love. For at the words of the Apostle Peter also, Ananias and his wife, as we read in the Acts of the Apostles, fell down dead, and were not raised to life again, but buried.

But if the heretics who are opposed to the Old Testament[194] will not credit this book, let them contemplate the Apostle Paul, whose writings they read along with us, saying with respect to a certain sinner whom he delivered over to Satan for the destruction of the flesh, "that the spirit may be saved."[195] And if they will not here understand death (for perhaps it is uncertain), let them acknowledge that punishment [requital] of some kind or other was inflicted by the apostle through the instrumentality of Satan; and that he did this not in hatred, but in love, is made plain by that addition, "that the spirit may be saved." Or let them notice what we say in those books to which they themselves attribute great authority, where it is written that the Apostle

---

193 Acts ii. 1-4.

194 *i.e.*, The Manicheans.

195 1 Cor. v. 5.

Thomas imprecated on a certain man, by whom he had been struck with the palm of the hand, the punishment of death in a very cruel form, while yet commending his soul to God, that it might be spared in the world to come,—whose hand, torn from the rest of his body after he had been killed by a lion, a dog brought to the table at which the apostle was feasting. It is allowable for us not to credit this writing, for it is not in the catholic canon; yet they both read it, and honour it as being thoroughly uncorrupted and thoroughly truthful, who rage very fiercely (with I know not what blindness) against the corporeal punishments which are in the Old Testament, being altogether ignorant in what spirit and at what stage in the orderly distribution of times they were inflicted.

Hence, in this class of injuries which is atoned for by punishment, such a measure will be preserved by Christians, that, on an injury being received, the mind will not mount up into hatred, but will be ready, in compassion for the infirmity, to endure even more; nor will it neglect the correction, which it can employ either by advice, or by authority, or by [the exercise of] power. There is another class of injuries, where complete restitution is possible, of which there are two species: the one referring to money, the other to labour.

And therefore examples are subjoined: of the former in the case of the coat and cloak, of the latter in the case of the compulsory service of one and two miles; for a garment may be given back, and he whom you have assisted by labour may also assist you, if it should be necessary. Unless, perhaps, the distinction should rather be drawn in this way: that the first case which is supposed, in reference to the cheek being struck, means all injuries that are inflicted by the wicked in such a way that restitution cannot be made except by punishment; and that the second case which is supposed, in reference to the garment, means all injuries where restitution can be made without punishment; and therefore, perhaps, it is added, "if any man will sue thee at the law," because what is taken away by means of a judicial sentence is not supposed to be taken away with such a degree of violence as that punishment is due; but that the third case is composed of both, so that restitution may be made both without punishment and with it. For the man who violently exacts labour to which he has no claim, without any judicial process, as he does who wickedly compels a man to go with him, and forces in an unlawful way assistance to be rendered to himself by one who is unwilling, is able both to pay the penalty of his wickedness and to repay the labour, if he who endured the wrong should ask it again. In all these classes of injuries, therefore, the Lord teaches that the disposition of a Christian ought to be most patient and compassionate, and thoroughly prepared to endure more.

But since it is a small matter merely to abstain from injuring, unless you also confer a benefit as far as you can, He therefore goes on to say, "Give to every one that asketh thee, and from him that would borrow of thee turn not thou away." "To every one that asketh," says He; not, Everything to him that asketh: so that you are to give that which you can honestly and justly give. For what if he should ask money, wherewith he may endeavour to oppress an innocent man? what if, in short, he should ask something unchaste?[196] But not to recount many examples, which are in fact innumerable, that certainly is to be given which may hurt neither thyself nor the other party, as far as can be known or supposed by man; and in the case of him to whom you have justly denied what he asks, justice itself is to be made known, so that you may not send him away

---

196 "To give everything to every one—the sword to the madman, the alms to the impostor, the criminal request to the temptress— would be to act as the enemy of others and ourselves" (Alford). Paul's *willingness* to spend and be spent illustrates a proper conformity to the precept.

empty. Thus you will give to every one that asketh you, although you will not always give what he asks; and you will sometimes give something better, when you have set him right who was making unjust requests.

Then, as to what He says, "From him that would borrow of thee turn not thou away," it is to be referred to the mind; for God loveth a cheerful giver.[197] Moreover, every one who accepts anything borrows, even if he himself is not going to pay it; for inasmuch as God pays back more to the merciful, whosoever does a kindness lends at interest. Or if it does not seem good to understand the borrower in any other sense than of him who accepts of anything with the intention of repaying it, we must understand the Lord to have included those two methods of doing a favour. For we either give in a present what we give in the exercise of benevolence, or we lend to one who will repay us. And frequently men who, setting before them the divine reward, are prepared to give away in a present, become slow to give what is asked in loan, as if they were destined to get nothing in return from God, inasmuch as he who receives pays back the thing which is given him. Rightly, therefore, does the divine authority exhort us to this

---

197 2 Cor. ix. 7.

mode of bestowing a favour, saying, "And from him that would borrow of thee turn not thou away:" *i.e.*, do not alienate your goodwill from him who asks it, both because your money will be useless, and because God will not pay you back, inasmuch as the man has done so; but when you do that from a regard to God's precept, it cannot be unfruitful with Him who gives these commands.[198]

---

198 This section, which concerns the *law of retaliation*, grew out of a rule of everyday life which the Pharisees constructed upon a principle of judicature laid down, Exod. xxi. 24 (Tholuck). The spirit, not the exact letter, of the illustrations is to be observed, and, when the spirit of the precept would demand it, the exact letter. Christians are taught to bear witness by enduring, yielding, and giving. "Sin is to be conquered by being made to feel the power of goodness." Christ gave a good example at His trial, without following the letter of His precept here; and Paul followed Him (1 Cor. iv. 12, 13).

Chapter XXI

In the next place, He goes on to say, "Ye have heard that it hath been said, Thou shalt love thy neighbour, and hate thine enemy: But I say unto you, Love your enemies, do good to them that hate you, and pray for them which persecute you;[199] that ye may be the children of your Father which is in heaven: for He commandeth[200] His sun to rise on the evil and on the good, and sendeth rain on the just and on the unjust. For if ye love[201] them which love you, what reward have ye? Do not even the publicans the same? And if ye salute your brethren only, what do ye more than others? Do not even the Gentiles the very same?[202] Be ye therefore perfect, even as your

---

199 Augustine, with the best Greek text, omits *et calumniantibus vos* ("and despitefully use you") of the Vulgate.

200 *Jubet*; Vulgate, *facit* (with the Greek).

201 *Dilexeritis*; Vulgate, *diligitis*.

202 *Hoc ipsum*; Vulgate, *hoc*; Greek, τὸ αὐτό.

Father who is in heaven[203] is perfect." For without this
love, wherewith we are commanded to love even our
enemies and persecutors, who can fully carry out those
things which are mentioned above? Moreover, the perfection of that mercy, wherewith most of all the soul that
is in distress is cared for, cannot be stretched beyond the
love of an enemy; and therefore the closing words are:
"Be ye therefore perfect, even as your Father who is in
heaven is perfect." Yet in such a way that God is understood to be perfect as God, and the soul to be perfect as
a soul.

That there is, however, a certain step [in advance]
in the righteousness of the Pharisees, which belongs to
the old law, is perceived from this consideration, that
many men hate even those by whom they are loved; as,
for instance, luxurious children hate their parents for
restraining them in their luxury. That man therefore
rises a certain step, who loves his neighbour, although
as yet he hates his enemy. But in the kingdom of Him
who came to fulfil the law, not to destroy it, he will
bring benevolence and kindness to perfection, when he
has carried it out so far as to love an enemy. For the
former stage, although it is something, is yet so little

---

203 *Qui est in cœlis*; Vulgate, *cœlestis* (see Revised Version).

that it may be reached even by the publicans as well. And as to what is said in the law, "Thou shalt hate thine enemy,"[204] it is not to be understood as the voice of

---

[204] The first part of the Lord's quotation is found in Lev. xix. 18; these words, whatever may be said about the sanction, real or apparent, of revenge and triumph over an enemy's fall in the Old Testament, are not found there. Bengel well says *pessima glossa* ("wretched gloss"),—a gloss of the Pharisees, "bearing plainly enough the character of post-exilic Judaism in its exclusiveness toward all surrounding nations" (Weiss). Centuries after Christ spoke these words, Maimonides gives utterance to this narrow feeling of hate: "If a Jew see a Gentile fall into the sea, let him by no means take him out; for it is written, 'Thou shalt love thy neighbour's blood,' but this is not thy neighbour." The separation of the Jews, demanded by their theocratic position, was the explanation in part—not an excuse—for such feeling towards people of other nationalities. Heathen peoples had the same feeling towards enemies. "It was the celebrated felicity of Sulla; and this was the crown of Xenophon's panegyric of Cyrus the Younger, that no one had done more good to his friends or more mischief to his enemies." Plautus said, "Man is a wolf to the stranger" ("*homo homini ignoto lupus est*"). The term "stranger" in Greek means "enemy." But common as this philosophy was to the pre-Christian world, the Jew was specially known for his hatred of all not of his own nationality (Juvenal, *Sat.* xiv. 104, etc.). The "enemy" referred to in the passage is not a national enemy (Keim) but a personal one (Weiss, Meyer, etc.). Our Lord subsequently defined who was to be understood by the term "neighbour" in the parable of the Good Samaritan (Luke x. 36).

command addressed to a righteous man, but rather as the voice of permission to a weak man.

Here indeed arises a question in no way to be blinked, that to this precept of the Lord, wherein He exhorts us to love our enemies, and to do good to those who hate us, and to pray for those who persecute us, many other parts of Scripture seem to those who consider them less diligently and soberly to stand opposed; for in the prophets there are found many imprecations against enemies, which are thought to be curses: as, for instance, that one, "Let their table become a snare,"[205] and the other things which are said there; and that one, "Let his children be fatherless, and his wife a widow,"[206] and the other statements which are made either before or afterwards in the same Psalm by the prophet, as bearing on the case of Judas. Many other statements are found in all parts of Scripture, which may seem contrary both to this precept of the Lord, and to that apostolic one, where it is said, "Bless; and curse not;"[207] while it is both written of the Lord, that He cursed the cities which received not His word;[208] and the above-

---

205 Ps. lxix. 22.

206 Ps. cix. 9.

207 Rom. xii. 14.

208 Matt. xi. 20, Luke x. 13.

mentioned apostle thus spoke respecting a certain man, "The Lord will reward him according to his works."[209]

But these difficulties are easily solved, for the prophet predicted by means of imprecation what was about to happen, not as praying for what he wished, but in the spirit of one who saw it beforehand. So also the Lord, so also the apostle; although even in the words of these we do not find what they have wished, but what they have foretold. For when the Lord says, "Woe unto thee, Capernaum," He does not utter anything else than that some evil will happen to her as a punishment of her unbelief; and that this would happen the Lord did not malevolently wish, but saw by means of His divinity. And the apostle does not say, May [the Lord] reward; but, "The Lord will reward him according to his work;" which is the word of one who foretells, not of one uttering an imprecation. Just as also, in regard to that hypocrisy of the Jews of which we have already spoken, whose destruction he saw to be impending, he said," God shall smite thee, thou whited wall."[210] But the prophets especially are

---

[209] 2 Tim. iv. 14. Augustine here again follows the better text than the *Textus Receptus*; so also Vulgate, *reddet*. See Revised Version.

[210] See above chap. xix.

accustomed to predict future events under the figure of one uttering an imprecation, just as they have often foretold those things which were to come under the figure of past time: as is the case, for example, in that passage, "Why have the nations raged, and the peoples imagined vain things?"[211] For he has not said, Why will the heathen rage, and the people imagine vain things? although he was not mentioning those things as if they were already past, but was looking forward to them as yet to come. Such also is that passage, "They have parted my garments among them, and have cast lots upon my vesture:"[212] for here also he has not said, They will part my garments among them, and will cast lots upon my vesture. And yet no one finds fault with these words, except the man who does not perceive that variety of figures in speaking in no degree lessens the truth of facts, and adds very much to the impressions on our minds.

---

211 Ps. ii. 1. The English version employs the present tense.
212 Ps. xxii. 18.

CHAPTER XXII

B ut the question before us is rendered more urgent by what the Apostle John says: "If any man see his brother sin a sin which is not unto death, he shall ask, and the Lord shall give him life for him who sinneth not unto death. There is a sin unto death: I do not say that he shall pray for it."[213] For he manifestly shows that there are certain brethren for whom we are not commanded to pray, although the Lord bids us pray even for our persecutors. Nor can the question in hand be solved, unless we acknowledge that there are certain sins in brethren which are more heinous than the persecution of enemies. Moreover, that brethren mean Christians can be proved by many examples from the divine Scriptures. Yet that one is plainest which the apostle thus states: "For the unbelieving husband is sanctified in the wife, and the unbelieving wife is sanctified in

---

213 1 John v. 16.

the brother."[214] For he has not added the word *our*; but has thought it plain, as he wished a Christian who had an unbelieving wife to be understood by the expression *brother*. And therefore he says a little after, "But if the unbelieving depart, let him depart: a brother or a sister is not under bondage in such cases."[215] Hence I am of opinion that the sin of a brother is unto death, when any one, after coming to the knowledge of God through the grace of our Lord Jesus Christ, makes an assault on the brotherhood, and is impelled by the fires of envy to oppose that grace itself by which he is reconciled to God. But the sin is not unto death, if any one has not withdrawn his love from a brother, but through some infirmity of disposition has failed to perform the incumbent duties of brotherhood. And on this account our Lord also on the cross says, "Father, forgive[216] them; for they know not what they do:"[217] for, not yet having become partakers of the grace of the Holy Spirit, they had not yet entered the fellowship of the holy brotherhood. And the blessed Stephen in the Acts of the Apostles prays for those by whom he

---

214 See note p.

215 1 Cor. vii. 14, 15.

216 *Ignosce*; Vulgate, *dimitte*.

217 Luke xxiii. 34.

is being stoned,[218] because they had not yet believed on Christ, and were not fighting against that common grace. And the Apostle Paul on this account, I believe, does not pray for Alexander, because he was already a brother, and had sinned unto death, viz. by making an assault on the brotherhood through envy. But for those who had not broken off their love, but had given way through fear, he prays that they may be pardoned. For thus he expresses it: "Alexander the coppersmith did me much evil: the Lord will reward him according to his works. Of whom be thou ware also; for he hath greatly withstood our words."[219] Then he adds for whom he prays, thus expressing it: "At my first defence no man stood with me, but all men forsook me: I pray God that it may not be laid to their charge."[220]

It is this difference in their sins which separates Judas the betrayer from Peter the denier: not that a penitent is not to be pardoned, for we must not come into collision with that declaration of our Lord, where He enjoins that a brother is to be pardoned, when he asks his brother to pardon him;[221] but that the ruin connected with that

---

218 Acts vii. 60.

219 *Sermonibus*; Vulgate, *verbis*.

220 2 Tim. iv. 14-16.

221 Matt. xviii. 21, Luke xvii. 3.

sin is so great, that he cannot endure the humiliation of asking for it, even if he should be compelled by a bad conscience both to acknowledge and divulge his sin. For when Judas had said, "I have sinned, in that I have betrayed the innocent blood," yet it was easier for him in despair to run and hang himself,[222] than in humility to ask for pardon. And therefore it is of much consequence to know what sort of repentance God pardons. For many much more readily confess that they have sinned, and are so angry with themselves that they vehemently wish they had not sinned; but yet they do not condescend to humble the heart and to make it contrite, and to implore pardon: and this disposition of mind we must suppose them to have, as feeling themselves already condemned because of the greatness of their sin.

And this is perhaps the sin against the Holy Ghost, *i.e.* through malice and envy to act in opposition to brotherly love after receiving the grace of the Holy Ghost,—a sin which our Lord says is not forgiven either in this world or in the world to come. And hence it may be asked whether the Jews sinned against the Holy Ghost, when they said that our Lord was casting out devils by Beelzebub, the prince of the devils:

---

222 Matt. xxvii. 4, 5.

whether we are to understand this as said against our Lord Himself, because He says of Himself in another passage, "If they have called the Master of the house Beelzebub, how much more shall they call them of His household!"[223] or whether, inasmuch as they had spoken from great envy, being ungrateful for so manifest benefits, although they were not yet Christians, they are, from the very greatness of their envy, to be supposed to have sinned against the Holy Ghost? This latter is certainly not to be gathered from our Lord's words. For although He has said in the same passage, "And whosoever speaketh a word against the Son of man, it shall be forgiven him; but whosoever speaketh a word against the Holy Ghost, it shall not be forgiven him, neither in this world, neither in the world to come;" yet it may seem that He admonished them for this purpose, that they should come to His grace, and after accepting of it should not so sin as they have now sinned. For now they have spoken a word against the Son of man, and it may be forgiven them, if they be converted, and believe on Him, and receive the Holy Ghost; but if, after receiving Him, they should choose to envy the brotherhood, and to assail the grace they

223 Matt. x. 25.

have received, it cannot be forgiven them, neither in this world nor in the world to come. For if He reckoned them so condemned, that there was no hope left for them, He would not judge that they ought still to be admonished, as He did by adding the statement, "Either make the tree good, and his fruit good; or else make the tree corrupt, and his fruit corrupt."[224]

Let it be understood, therefore, that we are to love our enemies, and to do good to those who hate us, and to pray for those who persecute us, in such a way, that it is at the same time understood that there are certain sins of brethren for which we are not commanded to pray; lest, through unskilfulness on our part, divine Scripture should seem to contradict itself (a thing which cannot happen). But whether, as we are not to pray for certain parties, so we are also to pray against some, has not yet become sufficiently evident. For it is said in general, "Bless, and curse not;" and again, "Recompense to no man evil for evil."[225] Moreover, while you do not pray for one, you do not therefore pray against him: for you may see that his punishment is certain, and his salvation altogether hopeless; and you do not pray for him, not because you hate him, but because you feel

---

224 Matt. xii. 24-33.
225 Rom. xii. 14, 17.

you can profit him nothing, and you do not wish your prayer to be rejected by the most righteous Judge. But what are we to think respecting those parties against whom we have it revealed that prayers were offered by the saints, not that they might be turned from their error (for in this way prayer is offered rather for them), but that final condemnation might come upon them: not as it was offered against the betrayer of our Lord by the prophet; for that, as has been said, was a prediction of things to come, not a wish for punishment: nor as it was offered by the apostle against Alexander; for respecting that also enough has been already said: but as we read in the Apocalypse of John of the martyrs praying that they may be avenged;[226] while the well known first martyr prayed that those who stoned him should be pardoned.

But we need not be moved by this circumstance. For who would venture to affirm, in regard to those white-robed saints, when they pleaded that they should be avenged, whether they pleaded against the men themselves or against the dominion of sin? For of itself it is a genuine avenging of the martyrs, and one full of righteousness and mercy, that the dominion of

---

226 Rev. vi. 10.

sin should be overthrown, under which dominion they were subjected to so great sufferings. And for its overthrow the apostle strives, saying, "Let not sin therefore reign in your mortal body."[227] But the dominion of sin is destroyed and overthrown, partly by the amendment of men, so that the flesh is brought under subjection to the spirit; partly by the condemnation of those who persevere in sin, so that they are righteously disposed of in such a way that they cannot be troublesome to the righteous who reign with Christ. Look at the Apostle Paul; does it not seem to you that he avenges the martyr Stephen in his own person, when he says: "So fight I, not as one that beateth the air: but I keep under my body, and bring it into subjection"?[228] For he was certainly laying prostrate, and weakening, and bringing into subjection, and regulating that principle in himself whence he had persecuted Stephen and the other Christians. Who then can demonstrate that the holy martyrs were not asking from the Lord such an avenging of themselves, when at the same time, in order to their being avenged, they might lawfully wish for the end of this world, in which they had endured

---

227 Rom. vi. 12.

228 1 Cor. ix. 26, 27. *Sevituti subjicio*; Vulgate, *in servitutem redigo*.

such martyrdoms? And they who pray for this, on the one hand pray for their enemies who are curable, and on the other hand do not pray against those who have chosen to be incurable: because God also, in punishing them, is not a malevolent Torturer, but a most righteous Disposer. Without any hesitation, therefore, let us love our enemies, let us do good to those that hate us, and let us pray for those who persecute us.

Chapter XXIII

Then, as to the statement which follows, "that ye may be the children of your Father which is in heaven,"[229] it is to be understood according to that rule in virtue of which John also says, "He gave them power to become the sons of God."[230] For one is a Son by nature, who knows nothing at all of sin; but we, by receiving power, are made sons, in as far as we perform those things which are commanded us by Him. And hence the apostolic teaching gives the name of adoption to that by which we are called to an eternal inheritance, that we may be joint heirs with Christ.[231] We are therefore made sons by a spiritual regeneration, and we are adopted into the kingdom

---

229 "Not in power or wisdom,—which was the cause of man's fall, and leads evermore to the same,—but in love" (Plumptre).
230 John i. 12.
231 Rom. viii. 17, Gal. iv. 5.

of God, not as aliens, but as being made and created by Him: so that it is one benefit, His having brought us into being through His omnipotence, when before we were nothing; another, His having adopted us, so that, as being sons, we might enjoy along with Him eternal life for our participation. Therefore He does not say, Do those things, because ye are sons; but, Do those things, that ye may be sons.

But when He calls us to this by the Only begotten Himself, He calls us to His own likeness. For He, as is said in what follows, "maketh[232] His sun to rise on the evil and on the good, and sendeth rain on the just and on the unjust." Whether you are to understand His sun as being not that which is visible to the fleshly eyes, but that wisdom of which it is said, "She is the brightness of the everlasting light;"[233] of which it is also said, "The Sun of righteousness has arisen upon me;" and again, "But unto you that fear the name of the Lord shall the Sun of righteousness arise:"[234] so that you would also

---

232 *Facit* (above, *jubet*). Bengel's comment is good: "*Magnifica appellatio. Ipse et fecit solem et gubernat et habet in sua unius potestate*" ("Splendid designation. He made the sun, governs it, and has it in His own power").

233 Wisdom vii. 26.

234 Mal. iv. 2.

understand the rain as being the watering with the
doctrine of truth, because Christ hath appeared to the
good and the evil, and is preached to the good and
the evil. Or whether you choose rather to understand
that sun which is set forth before the bodily eyes not
only of men, but also of cattle; and that rain by which
the fruits are brought forth, which have been given for
the refreshment of the body, which I think is the more
probable interpretation: so that that spiritual sun does
not rise except on the good and holy; for it is this very
thing which the wicked bewail in that book which is
called the Wisdom of Solomon, "And the sun rose not
upon us:"[235] and that spiritual rain does not water any
except the good; for the wicked were meant by the
vineyard of which it is said, "I will also command my
clouds that they rain no rain upon it."[236] But whether
you understand the one or the other, it takes place by
the great goodness of God, which we are commanded
to imitate, if we wish to be the children of God. For
who is there so ungrateful as not to feel how great the
comfort, so far as this life is concerned, which that visible light and the material rain bring? And this comfort
we see bestowed in this life alike upon the righteous

---

235 Wisdom v. 6.
236 Isa. v. 6.

and upon sinners in common. But He does not say, "who maketh the sun to rise on the evil and on the good;" but He has added the word "His," *i.e.* which He Himself made and established, and for the making of which He took nothing from any one, as it is written in Genesis respecting all the luminaries;[237] and He can properly say that all the things which He has created out of nothing are His own: so that we are hence admonished with how great liberality we ought, according to His precept, to give to our enemies those things which we have not created, but have received from His gifts.

But who can either be prepared to bear injuries from the weak, in as far as it is profitable for their salvation; and to choose rather to suffer more injustice from another than to repay what he has suffered; to give to every one that asketh anything from him, either what he asks, if it is in his possession, and if it can rightly be given, or good advice, or to manifest a benevolent disposition, and not to turn away from him who desires to borrow; to love his enemies, to do good to those who hate him, to pray for those who persecute him;—who, I say, does these things, but the man who is fully and

---

237 Gen. i. 16.

perfectly merciful?[238] And with that counsel misery is
avoided, by the assistance of Him who says, "I desire

---

238 "Be ye therefore perfect, as your heavenly Father is perfect."
The Greek text has here the future: ἐσεσθε τέλειοι, "Ye therefore
shall be perfect" (Revised Version). Meyer gives the verb the imperative sense; Alford, Lange, and others include the imperative
sense. The imperative force adds not a little to the plausibility of
deriving the doctrine of perfectibility on earth, or complete "sanc-
tification," from the passage, as the Pelagians (whom Augustine
elsewhere combats) and some Methodist commentators (Whe-
don, etc.). Alford, Trench, etc., deny that the verse gives any countenance to the doctrine. As regards the nature of the perfection,
Bengel sententiously says, "*in amore, erga omnes*" ("in love, toward
all." See Col. iii. 14). It seems "to refer chiefly to the perfection
of the divine love" (Mansel); so also Bleek, Meyer. Weiss (whose
Leben Jesu, i. 532–534, see) finds an allusion to the fundamental
command of the Old Testament, "Be ye holy," etc. In the place
of the divine holiness, or God's elevation above all uncleanness of
the creature, is substituted the divine perfection, whose essence is
all-comprehensive and unselfish love; and in the place of the God
separated from the sinful people, appears He who in love conde-
scends to them and brings them into likeness with Himself as His
children. The last verse of the Sermon as reported by Luke vi. 36
confirms the idea that the perfection is of love: "Be ye merciful, as
your Father which is in heaven is merciful." Commenting on this
verse, Dr. Schaff says, "Instruction in morality cannot rise above
this. Having thus led us up to our heavenly Father as the true
standard, our Lord, by a natural transition, passes to our religious
duties, *i.e.* duties to our heavenly Father."

mercy, and not sacrifice."[239] "Blessed," therefore, "are the merciful: for they shall obtain mercy." But now I think it will be more convenient, that at this point the reader, fatigued with so long a volume, should breathe a little, and recruit himself for considering what remains in another book.

---

239 Hos. vi. 6.

Book II

*On the latter part of our Lord's Sermon
on the Mount, contained in the sixth
and seventh chapters of Matthew.*

Chapter I

The subject of mercy, with the treatment of which the first book came to a close, is followed by that of the cleansing of the heart, with which the present one begins.[240] The cleansing of the heart, then, is as it were the cleansing of the eye by which God is seen; and in keeping that single, there ought to be as great care as the dignity of the object demands, which can be beheld by such an eye. But even when this eye is in great part cleansed, it is difficult to prevent certain defilements from creeping insensibly over it, from those things which are wont to accompany even our good actions,— as, for instance, the praise of men. If, indeed, not to live uprightly is hurtful; yet to live uprightly, and not to

---

240 Jesus passes from the precepts of the genuine righteousness to the actual practice of the same (Meyer, Weiss), from moral to religious duties (Lange), from actions to motives; having spoken to the heart before by inference, he now speaks directly (Alford).

wish to be praised, what else is this than to be an enemy
to the affairs of men, which are certainly so much the
more miserable, the less an upright life on the part of
men gives pleasure? If, therefore, those among whom
you live shall not praise you when living uprightly,
they are in error: but if they shall praise you, you are
in danger; unless you have a heart so single and pure,
that in those things in which you act uprightly you do
not so act because of the praises of men; and that you
rather congratulate those who praise what is right, as
having pleasure in what is good, than yourself; because
you would live uprightly even if no one were to praise
you: and that you understand this very praise of you to
be useful to those who praise you, only when it is not
yourself whom they honour in your good life, but God,
whose most holy temple every man is who lives well; so
that what David says finds its fulfilment, "In the Lord
shall my soul be praised; the humble shall hear thereof,
and be glad."[241] It belongs therefore to the pure eye not
to look at the praises of men in acting rightly, nor to
have reference to these while you are acting rightly, *i.e.*
to do anything rightly with the very design of pleasing
men. For thus you will be disposed also to counterfeit

---

241 Ps. xxxiv. 2.

what is good, if nothing is kept in view except the praise of man; who, inasmuch as he cannot see the heart, may also praise things that are false. And they who do this, *i.e.* who counterfeit goodness, are of a double heart. No one therefore has a single, *i.e.* a pure heart, except the man who rises above the praises of men; and when he lives well, looks at Him only, and strives to please Him who is the only Searcher of the conscience. And whatever proceeds from the purity of that conscience is so much the more praiseworthy, the less it desires the praises of men.

"Take heed,[242] therefore," says He, "that ye do not your righteousness[243] before men, to be seen of them:" *i.e.*, take heed that ye do not live righteously with this intent, and that ye do not place your happiness in this, that men may see you. "Otherwise ye have no reward of your Father who is in heaven:" not if ye should be seen by men; but if ye should live righteously with the intent of being seen by men. For, [were it the former], what would become of the statement made in

---

242 *Cavete facere*; Vulgate, *attendite ne faciatis.*

243 In agreement with the best Greek text. (See Revised Version.) This verse is a general proposition. The three leading manifestations of righteousness and practical piety among the Jews follow,—almsgiving, prayer, fasting.

the beginning of this sermon, "Ye are the light of the world. A city that is set on an hill cannot be hid. Neither do men light a candle, and put it under a bushel, but on a candlestick; and it giveth light unto all that are in the house. Let your light so shine before men, that they may see your good works"? But He did not set up this as the end; for He has added, "and glorify your Father who is in heaven."[244] But here, because he is finding fault with this, if the end of our right actions is there, *i.e.* if we act rightly with this design, only of being seen of men; after He has said, "Take heed that ye do not your righteousness before men," He has added nothing. And hereby it is evident that He has said this, not to prevent us from acting rightly before men, but lest perchance we should act rightly before men for the purpose of being seen by them, *i.e.* should fix our eye on this, and make it the end of what we have set before us.

For the apostle also says, "If I yet pleased men, I should not be the servant of Christ;"[245] while he says in another place, "Please all men in all things, even as I also please all men in all things."[246] And they who do

---

244 Matt. v. 14-16.
245 Gal. i. 10.
246 1 Cor. x. 32, 33.

not understand this think it a contradiction; while the explanation is, that he has said he does not please men, because he was accustomed to act rightly, not with the express design of pleasing men, but of pleasing God, to the love of whom he wished to turn men's hearts by that very thing in which he was pleasing men. Therefore he was both right in saying that he did not please men, because in that very thing he aimed at pleasing God: and right in authoritatively teaching that we ought to please men, not in order that this should be sought for as the reward of our good deeds; but because the man who would not offer himself for imitation to those whom he wished to be saved, could not please God; but no man possibly can imitate one who has not pleased him. As, therefore, that man would not speak absurdly who should say, In this work of seeking a ship, it is not a ship, but my native country, that I seek: so the apostle also might fitly say, In this work of pleasing men, it is not men, but God, that I please; because I do not aim at pleasing men, but have it as my object, that those whom I wish to be saved may imitate me. Just as he says of an offering that is made for the saints, "Not because I desire a gift, but I desire fruit;"[247] *i.e.*,

---

247 Phil. iv. 17.

In seeking your gift, I seek not it, but your fruit. For by this proof it could appear how far they had advanced Godward, when they offered that willingly which was sought from them not for the sake of his own joy over their gifts, but for the sake of the fellowship of love.

Although when He also goes on to say, "Otherwise ye have no reward of your Father who is in heaven,"[248] He points out nothing else but that we ought to be on our guard against seeking man's praise as the reward of our deeds, *i.e.* against thinking we thereby attain to blessedness.

---

248 Acts otherwise noble and praiseworthy become sin when done to make an appearance before men, and get honour from them. Bad intentions vitiate pious observances.

Chapter II

"Therefore, when thou doest thine alms," says He, "do not sound a trumpet before thee, as the hypocrites do in the synagogues and in the streets, that they may have glory[249] of men." Do not, says He, desire to become known in the same way as the hypocrites. Now it is manifest that hypocrites have not that in their heart also which they hold forth before the eyes of men. For hypocrites are pretenders, as it were setters forth of other characters, just as in the plays of the theatre. For he who acts the part of Agamemnon in tragedy, for example, or of any other person belonging to the history or legend which is acted, is not really

---

249 *Glorificantur;* Vulgate *honorificentur.* The sounding of trumpet is referred by some to an alleged custom of the parties themselves calling the poor together by a trumpet, or even to the noise of the coins on the trumpet-shaped chests in the temple. Better, it is figurative of "self-laudation and display" (Meyer, Alford, Lange, etc.).

the person himself, but personates him, and is called a hypocrite. In like manner, in the Church, or in any phase of human life, whoever wishes to seem what he is not is a hypocrite. For he pretends, but does not show himself, to be a righteous man; because he places the whole fruit [of his acting] in the praise of men, which even pretenders may receive, while they deceive those to whom they seem good, and are praised by them. But such do not receive a reward from God the Searcher of the heart, unless it be the punishment of their deceit: from men, however, says He, "They have received their reward;" and most righteously will it be said to them, Depart from me, ye workers of deceit; ye had my name, but ye did not my works. Hence they have received their reward, who do their alms for no other reason than that they may have glory of men; not if they have glory of men, but if they do them for the express purpose of having this glory, as has been discussed above. For the praise of men ought not to be sought by him who acts rightly, but ought to follow him who acts rightly, so that they may profit who can also imitate what they praise, not that he whom they praise may think that they are profiting him anything.

"But when thou doest alms, let not thy left hand know what thy right hand doeth." If you should understand unbelievers to be meant by the left hand, then it will seem to be no fault to wish to please believers; while nevertheless we are altogether prohibited from placing the fruit and end of our good deed in the praise of any men whatever. But as regards this point, that those who have been pleased with your good deeds should imitate you, we are to act before the eyes not only of believers, but also of unbelievers, so that by our good works, which are to be praised, they may honour God, and may come to salvation. But if you should be of opinion that the left hand means an enemy, so that your enemy is not to know when you do alms, why did the Lord Himself, when His enemies the Jews were standing round, mercifully heal men? why did the Apostle Peter, by healing the lame man whom he pitied at the gate Beautiful, bring also the wrath of the enemy upon himself, and upon the other disciples of Christ?[250] Then, further, if it is necessary that the enemy should not know when we do our alms, how shall we do with the enemy himself so as to fulfil that precept, "If thine enemy be hungry, give him bread to eat; and if he be thirsty, give him water to drink"?[251]

A third opinion is wont to be held by carnal people, so absurd and ridiculous, that I would not mention it had I not found that not a few are entangled in that

---

250 Acts iii. 0, Acts iv. 0.

251 Prov. xxv. 21.

error, who say that by the expression left hand a wife
is meant; so that, inasmuch as in family affairs women
are wont to be more tenacious of money, it is to be kept
hid from them when their husbands compassionately
spend anything upon the needy, for fear of domestic
quarrels. As if, forsooth, men alone were Christians,
and this precept were not addressed to women also!
From what left hand, then, is a woman enjoined to
conceal her deed of mercy? Is a husband also the left
hand of his wife? A statement most absurd. Or if any
one thinks that they are left hands to each other; if any
part of the family property be expended by the one
party in such a way as to be contrary to the will of
the other party, such a marriage will not be a Christian
one; but whichever of them should choose to do alms
according to the command of God, whomsoever he
should find opposed, would inevitably be an enemy to
the command of God, and therefore reckoned among
unbelievers,—the command with respect to such parties being, that a believing husband should win his
wife, and a believing wife her husband, by their good
conversation and conduct; and therefore they ought
not to conceal their good works from each other, by
which they are to be mutually attracted, so that the
one may be able to attract the other to communion

in the Christian faith. Nor are thefts to be perpetrated in order that God may be rendered propitious. But if anything is to be concealed as long as the infirmity of the other party is unable to bear with equanimity what nevertheless is not done unjustly and unlawfully; yet, that the left hand is not meant in such a sense on the present occasion, readily appears from a consideration of the whole section, whereby it will at the same time be discovered what He calls the left hand.

"Take heed," says He, "that ye do not your righteousness before men, to be seen of them; otherwise ye have no reward of your Father which is in heaven." Here He has mentioned righteousness generally, then He follows it up in detail. For a deed which is done in the way of alms is a certain part of righteousness, and therefore He connects the two by saying, "Therefore, when thou doest thine alms, do not sound a trumpet before thee, as the hypocrites do in the synagogues and in the streets, that they may have glory of men." In this there is a reference to what He says before, "Take heed that ye do not your righteousness before men, to be seen of them." But what follows, "Verily I say unto you, They have received their reward," refers to that other statement which He has made above, "Otherwise ye have no reward of your Father which is in heaven." Then follows, "But when thou doest alms."

When He says, "But thou," what else does He mean but, Not in the same manner as they? What, then, does He bid me do? "But when thou doest alms," says He, "let not thy left hand know what thy right hand doeth." Hence those other parties so act, that their left hand knoweth what their right hand doeth. What, therefore, is blamed in them, this thou art forbidden to do. But this is what is blamed in them, that they act in such a way as to seek the praises of men. And therefore the left hand seems to have no more suitable meaning than just this delight in praise. But the right hand means the intention of fulfilling the divine commands. When, therefore, with the consciousness of him who does alms is mixed up the desire of man's praise, the left hand becomes conscious of the work of the right hand: "Let not, therefore, thy left hand know what thy right hand doeth;"[252] *i.e.* Let there not be mixed up in thy consciousness the desire of man's praise, when in doing alms thou art striving to fulfil a divine command.

---

252 "With complete modesty; secret, noiseless giving" (Chrysostom). No reference to a counting of the money by the left hand (Paulus, De Wette). Luther's comment is quaint and characteristic: "When thou givest alms with thy right hand, take heed that thou dost not seek with the left to take more, but put it behind thy back." Trench pronounces this discussion concerning the meaning of the *left hand* "laborious, and, as I cannot but think, unnecessary;" but it is ingenious and interesting.

"That thine alms may be in secret."[253] What else is meant by "in secret," but just in a good conscience, which cannot be shown to human eyes, nor revealed by words? since, indeed, the mass of men tell many lies. And therefore, if the right hand acts inwardly in secret, all outward things, which are visible and temporal, belong to the left hand. Let thine alms, therefore, be in thine own consciousness, where many do alms by their good intention, even if they have no money or anything else which is to be bestowed on one who is needy. But many give alms outwardly, and not inwardly, who either from ambition, or for the sake of some temporal object, wish to appear merciful, in whom the left hand only is to be reckoned as working. Others again hold, as it were, a middle place between the two; so that, with a design which is directed Godward, they do their alms, and yet there insinuates itself into this excellent wish also some desire after praise, or after a perishable and temporal object of some sort or other. But our Lord much more strongly prohibits the left hand alone being at work in us, when He even forbids its being mixed up with the works of the right hand: that is to say, that we are not only to beware of doing alms from the desire of

---

253 *Pii lucent et tamen latent* (Bengel).

temporal objects alone; but that in this work we are not even to have regard to God in such a way as that there should be mingled up or united therewith the grasping after outward advantages. For the question under discussion is the cleansing of the heart, which, unless it be single, will not be clean. But how will it be single, if it serves two masters, and does not purge its vision by the striving after eternal things alone, but clouds it by the love of mortal and perishable things as well? "Let thine alms," therefore, "be in secret; and thy[254] Father, who seeth in secret, shall reward thee." Altogether most righteously and most truly. For if you expect a reward from Him who is the only Searcher of the conscience, let conscience itself suffice thee for meriting a reward. Many Latin copies have it thus, "And thy Father who seeth in secret shall reward thee openly;" but because we have not found the word "openly" in the Greek copies, which are earlier,[255] we have not thought that anything was to be said about it.

---

254   Not *our* Father.

255   It is wanting in the Sinaitic, B, D, etc., mss., as also in the Vulgate copies.

CHAPTER III

"And when ye pray," says He, "ye shall not be as the hypocrites are; for they love to pray standing[256] in the synagogues and in the corners of the streets, that they may be seen of men." And here also it is not the being seen of men that is wrong, but doing these things for the purpose of being seen of men; and it is superfluous to make the same remark so often, since there is just one rule to be kept, from which we learn that what we should dread and avoid is not that men know these things, but that they be done with this intent, that the fruit of pleasing men should be sought after in them. Our Lord Himself, too, preserves the same words, when He adds similarly, "Verily I say unto you, They

---

[256] They love to *stand* praying, more than they love to pray. Like the Mohammedans of today, they took delight in airing their piety. Our Lord mentions the most conspicuous localities. The usual posture of the Jews in prayer was standing (1 Sam. i. 26, Luke xviii. 11, etc.).

have received their reward;" hereby showing that He forbids this,—the striving after that reward in which fools delight when they are praised by men.

"But when ye[257] pray," says He, "enter into your bedchambers." What are those bedchambers but just our hearts themselves, as is meant also in the Psalm, when it is said, "What ye say in your hearts, have remorse for even in your beds"?[258] "And when ye have shut[259] the doors," says He, "pray to your Father who is in secret."[260] It is a small matter to enter into our bedchambers if the door stand open to the unmannerly, through which the things that are outside profanely rush in and assail our inner man. Now we have said that outside are all temporal and visible things, which make their way through the door, *i.e.* through the fleshly sense into our thoughts, and clamorously interrupt those who are praying by a crowd of vain phantoms. Hence the door is to be shut, *i.e.* the fleshly sense is to be resisted, so that spiritual prayer may be directed to the Father, which is done in the inmost heart, where

257 *Vos*; Vulgate, *tu* (Revised Version).

258 Ps. iv. 4. The English version renders, "Commune with your own heart upon your bed, and be still."

259 *Claudentes ostia*; Vulgate, *clauso ostio*.

260 Our Lord on occasion followed this habit (Matt. xiv. 23 and in Gethsemane).

prayer is offered to the Father which is in secret. "And your Father," says He, "who seeth in secret, shall reward you." And this had to be wound up with a closing statement of such a kind; for here at the present stage the admonition is not that we should pray, but as to how we should pray. Nor is what goes before an admonition that we should give alms, but as to the spirit in which we should do so, inasmuch as He is giving instructions with regard to the cleansing of the heart, which nothing cleanses but the undivided and single-minded striving after eternal life from the pure love of wisdom alone.

"But when ye pray," says He, "do not speak much,[261]

---

261 Greek, βατταλογεω "Use not vain repetitions," Revised Version (or *stammer*). Some derive the word from Battus, king of Cyrene, who stuttered, or from Battus, author of wordy poems. The word is probably only an imitation of the sound of the stammerer (Thayer, *Lexicon*, who spells βαττολογεω). The Jews were only doing as well as the Gentiles when they placed virtue in the length of the prayer, and no better. "Who makes his prayer long, shall not return home empty" (Rabbi Chasima, quoted by Hausrath, 73). The Rabbins took up at great length the question how many and what kind of petitions should be offered up at the table spread on different occasions with different viands, whether salutations should be acknowledged in the course of prayer, etc. (see Schürer, pp. 498, 499). Examples of repetitious prayer in Scripture: 1 Kings xviii. 26, Acts xix. 34. The warning is not against frequent prayer (Luke xviii. 1).

as the heathen do; for they think[262] that they shall be
heard for their much speaking." As it is characteristic
of the hypocrites to exhibit themselves to be gazed at
when praying, and their fruit is to please men, so it
is characteristic of the heathen, i.e. of the Gentiles, to
think they are heard for their much speaking. And in
reality, every kind of much speaking comes from the
Gentiles, who make it their endeavour to exercise the
tongue rather than to cleanse the heart. And this kind
of useless exertion they endeavour to transfer even to
the influencing of God by prayer, supposing that the
Judge, just like man, is brought over by words to a certain way of thinking. "Be not ye, therefore, like unto
them," says the only true Master. "For your Father
knoweth what things are necessary[263] for you, before ye
ask Him." For if many words are made use of with the
intent that one who is ignorant may be instructed and
taught, what need is there of them for Him who knows
all things, to whom all things which exist, by the very
fact of their existence, speak, and show themselves as
having been brought into existence; and those things
which are future do not remain concealed from His
knowledge and wisdom, in which both those things

---

262 *Arbitrantur*; Vulgate, *putant*.
263 *Vobis necessarium*; Vulgate, *opus*.

which are past, and those things which will yet come to pass, are all present and cannot pass away?

But since, however few they may be, yet there are words which He Himself also is about to speak, by which He would teach us to pray; it may be asked why even these few words are necessary for Him who knows all things before they take place, and is acquainted, as has been said, with what is necessary for us before we ask Him? Here, in the first place, the answer is, that we ought to urge our case with God, in order to obtain what we wish, not by words, but by the ideas which we cherish in our mind, and by the direction of our thought, with pure love and sincere desire; but that our Lord has taught us the very ideas in words, that by committing them to memory we may recollect those ideas at the time we pray.

But again, it may be asked (whether we are to pray in ideas or in words) what need there is for prayer itself, if God already knows what is necessary for us; unless it be that the very effort involved in prayer calms and purifies our heart, and makes it more capacious for receiving the divine gifts, which are poured into us spiritually.[264] For it is not on account of the urgency of our

264 The illustration is frequently used (M. Henry; after him F. W. Robertson), to represent the position of some, that prayer only has

prayers that God hears us, who is always ready to give us His light, not of a material kind, but that which is intellectual and spiritual: but we are not always ready to receive, since we are inclined towards other things, and are involved in darkness through our desire for temporal things. Hence there is brought about in prayer a turning of the heart to Him, who is ever ready to give, if we will but take what He has given; and in the very act of turning there is effected a purging of the inner eye, inasmuch as those things of a temporal kind which were desired are excluded, so that the vision of the pure heart may be able to bear the pure light, divinely shining, without any setting or change: and not only to bear it, but also to remain in it; not merely without annoyance, but also with ineffable joy, in which a life truly and sincerely blessed is perfected.

---

an influence on the petitioner, of a boatman in his boat, taking hold of the wharf with his grappling hook. While prayer does not "inform or persuade God," it is the condition of receiving. The sanctifying influence is secondary and incidental.

Chapter IV

B ut now we have to consider what things we are taught to pray for by Him through whom we both learn what we are to pray for, and obtain what we pray for. "After this manner, therefore, pray ye,"[265] says He: "Our Father who art in heaven, Hallowed be Thy name. Thy kingdom come. Thy will be done on earth, as it is in heaven. Give us this day our daily[266] bread. And forgive us our debts, as we forgive our debtors. And bring[267] us not into temptation, but deliver us from evil."[268] Seeing that in all prayer we have to

---

265 *Orate*; Vulgate, *Orabitis*.

266 *Quotidianum*; Vulgate, *supersubstantialem*.

267 *Inferas* (*Rev. Vers.*); Vulgate, *inducas*.

268 This prayer is called the Lord's Prayer because our Lord is its author, He did not and could not have used it Himself, on account of (1) the special meaning of the pronoun "our" in the address, (2) the confession of sins in the fifth petition. Luke's account (xi. 1) agrees in the subject of the petitions as in the address,

conciliate the goodwill of him to whom we pray, then

---

but differs (1) in the omission of the third petition (Crit text); (2) in the addition to the fifth petition (which, however, Matthew gives at the close of the prayer in a more elaborate form); (3) in adducing a request of the disciples as the occasion of the prayer. Some have thought the prayer was given on two occasions (Meyer in earlier edd., Tholuck). Others hold that Matthew has inserted it out of its proper historical place (Neander, Olshausen, De Wette, Ebrard, Meyer in ed. vi., Weiss, etc.). This question of priority and accuracy as between the forms of Matthew and Luke may be regarded as set at rest by the *Teaching of the Twelve Apostles*, which (viii. 2) gives the exact form of Matthew with three unimportant differences: viz. (1) *heaven*, οὐρανῷ, instead of *heavens*; (2) the omission of the article before *earth*; (3) *debt* instead of *debts*. This document contains the doxology (with the omission of *kingdom*), and supports the *Textus Receptus* in giving the present, *we forgive*, ἀφίεμεν, instead of the perfect, *we have forgiven*, ἀφῆκαμεν.— The *division* of the prayer is usually made into (1) address, (2) petitions, (3) doxology (omitted from the approved critical Greek text and the Revised Version).—The petitions are seven according to Augustine, Luther, Bengel, Tholuck, etc: six (the two last being combined as one) according to Chrysostom, Reformed catechisms, Calvin, Schaff, etc. The petitions are divided into two groups (Tertullian) or tables (Calvin).—The *contents* of the first three petitions concern the glory of God; of the last four, the wants of men. In the first group the pronoun is *thy*, and the direction of the thought is from heaven downwards to earth; in the second group it is *us*, and the direction of the thought is from earth upwards to God.—The numbers, in view of their significance in the Old Testament, 3, 4, 7, are not an uninteresting item.

to say what we pray for; goodwill is usually conciliated by our offering praise to him to whom the prayer is directed, and this is usually put in the beginning of the prayer: and in this particular our Lord has bidden us say nothing else but "Our Father who art in heaven." For many things are said in praise of God, which, being scattered variously and widely over all the Holy Scriptures, every one will be able to consider when he reads them: yet nowhere is there found a precept for the people of Israel, that they should say "Our Father," or that they should pray to God as a Father; but as Lord He

---

Tholuck says: "The attention of the student who has otherwise heard of the doctrine of the Trinity will find a distinct reference to it in the arrangement of this prayer. In the first petition of each group, God is referred to as Creator and Preserver; in the second as Redeemer; in the third as the Holy Spirit."—The Lord's Prayer is more than a specimen of prayer: it is a pattern. Different views are held concerning its liturgical use, which can be traced back to Cyprian and Tertullian, and now farther still, to the *Teaching of the Apostles*, which, after giving the prayer, says, "Thrice a day pray thus." It also gives (ix.) a form of prayer to be used after the Eucharist. Of its abuse Luther says, "It is the greatest martyr."—It is not a *compilation*, although similar or the same, petitions may have been in use among the Jews. The simplicity, symmetry of arrangement, depth and progress of thought, reverence of feeling, make it, indeed, the model prayer,—the Lord's Prayer. Tertullian calls it *breviarium totius evangelii* (so Meyer).

was made known to them, as being yet servants, *i.e.* still living according to the flesh. I say this, however, inasmuch as they received the commands of the law, which they were ordered to observe: for the prophets often show that this same Lord of ours might have been their Father also, if they had not strayed from His commandments: as, for instance, we have that statement, "I have nourished and brought up children, and they have rebelled against me;"[269] and that other, "I have said, Ye are gods; and all of you are children of the Most High;"[270] and this again, "If then I be a Father, where is mine honour? and if I be a Master, where is my fear?"[271] and very many other statements, where the Jews are accused of showing by their sin that they did not wish to become sons: those things being left out of account which are said in prophecy of a future Christian people, that they would have God as a Father, according to that gospel statement, "To them gave He power to become the sons of God."[272] The Apostle Paul, again, says, "The heir, as long as he is a child, differeth nothing from a

---

269 Isa. i. 2.
270 Ps. lxxxii. 6.
271 Mal. i. 6.
272 John i. 12.

servant;" and mentions that we have received the Spirit of adoption, "whereby we cry, Abba, Father."[273]

And since the fact that we are called to an eternal inheritance, that we might be fellow heirs with Christ and attain to the adoption of sons, is not of our deserts, but of God's grace; we put this very same grace in the beginning of our prayer, when we say "Our Father." And by that appellation both love is stirred up—for what ought to be dearer to sons than a father?—and a suppliant disposition, when men say to God, "Our Father:" and a certain presumption of obtaining what we are about to ask; since, before we ask anything, we have received so great a gift as to be allowed to call God "Our Father."[274] For what would He not now give to sons when they ask, when He has already granted this very thing, namely, that they might be sons? Lastly, how great solicitude takes hold of the mind, that he who says "Our Father," should not prove unworthy of so great a Father! For if any plebeian should be permitted by the party himself to call a senator of more advanced age father; without doubt he would tremble, and would not readily venture to do it, reflecting on the humbleness of his origin, and the scantiness of his

---

273 Rom. viii. 15, Gal. iv. 1.

274 *Patrem quisquis appellare potest, omnia orare potest* (Bengel).

resources, and the worthlessness of his plebeian person: how much more, therefore, ought we to tremble to call God Father, if there is so great a stain and so much baseness in our character, that God might much more justly drive forth these from contact with Himself, than that senator might the poverty of any beggar whatever! Since, indeed, he (the senator) despises that in the beggar to which even he himself may be reduced by the vicissitude of human affairs: but God never falls into baseness of character. And thanks be to the mercy of Him who requires this of us, that He should be our Father,—a relationship which can be brought about by no expenditure of ours, but solely by God's goodwill. Here also there is an admonition to the rich and to those of noble birth, so far as this world is concerned, that when they have become Christians they should not comport themselves proudly towards the poor and the low of birth; since together with them they call God "Our Father,"—an expression which they cannot truly and piously use, unless they recognise that they themselves are brethren.

Chapter V

Let the new people, therefore, who are called to an eternal inheritance, use the word of the New Testament, and say, "Our Father who art in heaven,"[275] *i.e.* in the holy and the just. For God is not contained in space. For the heavens are indeed the higher material bodies of the world, but yet material, and therefore cannot exist except in some definite place; but if God's place is believed to be in the heavens, as meaning the higher parts of the world, the birds are of greater value than we, for their life is nearer to God. But it is not written, The Lord is nigh unto tall men, or unto those who dwell on mountains; but it is written, "The Lord is nigh unto them that are of a broken heart,"[276] which

---

275 "The address puts us into the proper attitude of prayer. It indicates our filial relation to God as 'Father' (word of faith), fraternal relation to our fellow men ('our,' word of love), and our destination of 'heaven' (word of hope)."

276 Ps. xxxiv. 18.

refers rather to humility. But as a sinner is called earth, when it is said to him, "Earth thou art, and unto earth shalt thou return;"[277] so, on the other hand, a righteous man may be called heaven. For it is said to the righteous, "For the temple of God is holy, which temple ye are."[278] And therefore, if God dwells in His temple, and the saints are His temple, the expression "which art in heaven" is rightly used in the sense, which art in the saints. And most suitable is such a similitude, so that spiritually there may be seen to be as great a difference between the righteous and sinners, as there is materially between heaven and earth.

And for the purpose of showing this, when we stand at prayer, we turn to the east, whence the heaven rises: not as if God also were dwelling there, in the sense that He who is everywhere present, not as occupying space, but by the power of His majesty, had forsaken the other parts of the world; but in order that the mind may be admonished to turn to a more excellent nature, *i.e.* to God, when its own body, which is earthly, is turned to a more excellent body, *i.e.* to a heavenly one. It is also suitable for the different stages of religion, and expedient in the highest degree, that in the minds of all,

---

277 Gen. iii. 19.
278 1 Cor. iii. 17.

both small and great, there should be cherished worthy
conceptions of God. And therefore, as regards those
who as yet are taken up with the beauties that are seen,
and cannot think of anything incorporeal, inasmuch
as they must necessarily prefer heaven to earth, their
opinion is more tolerable, if they believe God, whom
as yet they think of after a corporeal fashion, to be in
heaven rather than upon earth: so that when at any future time they have learned that the dignity of the soul
exceeds even a celestial body, they may seek Him in
the soul rather than in a celestial body even; and when
they have learned how great a distance there is between
the souls of sinners and of the righteous, just as they
did not venture, when as yet they were wise only after
a carnal fashion, to place Him on earth, but in heav-
en, so afterwards with better faith or intelligence they
may seek Him again in the souls of the righteous rather
than in those of sinners. Hence, when it is said, "Our
Father which art in heaven," it is rightly understood to
mean in the hearts of the righteous, as it were in His
holy temple. And at the same time, in such a way that
he who prays wishes Him whom he invokes to dwell
in himself also; and when he strives after this, practises
righteousness,—a kind of service by which God is attracted to dwell in the soul.

Let us see now what things are to be prayed for. For it has been stated who it is that is prayed to, and where He dwells. First of all, then, of those things which are prayed for comes this petition, "Hallowed be Thy name." And this is prayed for, not as if the name of God were not holy already, but that it may be held holy by men; *i.e.*, that God may so become known to them, that they shall reckon nothing more holy, and which they are more afraid of offending. For, because it is said, "In Judah is God known; His name is great in Israel,"[279] we are not to understand the statement in this way, as if God were less in one place, greater in another; but there His name is great, where He is named according to the greatness of His majesty. And so there His name is said to be holy, where He is named with veneration and the fear of offending Him. And this is what is now going on, while the gospel, by becoming known everywhere throughout the different nations, commends the name of the one God by means of the administration of His Son.

---

279 Ps. lxxvi. 1.

CHAPTER VI

In the next place there follows, "Thy kingdom come." Just as the Lord Himself teaches in the Gospel that the day of judgment will take place at the very time when the gospel shall have been preached among all nations:[280] a thing which belongs to the hallowing of God's name. For here also the expression "Thy kingdom come" is not used in such a way as if God were not now reigning. But some one perhaps might say the expression "come" meant *upon earth*; as if, indeed, He were not even now really reigning upon earth, and had not always reigned upon it from the foundation of the world. "Come," therefore, is to be understood in the sense of "manifested to men." For in the same way also as a light which is present is absent to the blind, and to those who shut their eyes; so the kingdom of God, though it never departs from the earth, is yet absent to those who are ignorant of it. But

---

280 Matt. xxiv. 14.

no one will be allowed to be ignorant of the kingdom of God, when His Only begotten shall come from heaven, not only in a way to be apprehended by the understanding, but also visibly in the person of the Divine Man, in order to judge the quick and the dead. And after that judgment, *i.e.* when the process of distinguishing and separating the righteous from the unrighteous has taken place, God will so dwell in the righteous, that there will be no need for any one being taught by man, but all will be, as it is written, "taught of God."[281] Then will the blessed life in all its parts be perfected in the saints unto eternity, just as now the most holy and blessed heavenly angels are wise and blessed, from the fact that God alone is their light; because the Lord hath promised this also to His own: "In the resurrection," says He, "they will be as the angels in heaven."[282]

And therefore, after that petition where we say, "Thy kingdom come," there follows, "Thy will be done, as in heaven so in earth:" *i.e.*, just as Thy will is in the angels who are in heaven, so that they wholly cleave to Thee, and thoroughly enjoy Thee, no error beclouding their wisdom, no misery hindering their blessedness; so let it be done in Thy saints who are on earth, and

---

281 Isa. liv. 13, John vi. 45.
282 Matt. xxii. 30.

made from the earth, so far as the body is concerned, and who, although it is into a heavenly habitation and exchange, are yet to be taken from the earth. To this there is a reference also in that doxology of the angels, "Glory to God in the highest,[283] and on earth peace to men of goodwill:"[284] so that when our goodwill has gone before, which follows Him that calleth, the will of God is perfected in us, as it is in the heavenly angels; so that no antagonism stands in the way of our blessedness: and this is peace. "Thy will be done" is also rightly understood in the sense of, Let obedience be rendered to Thy precepts: "as in heaven so on earth," *i.e.* as by the angels so by men. For, that the will of God is done when His precepts are obeyed, the Lord Himself says, when He affirms, "My meat is to do the will of Him that sent me;"[285] and often, "I came, not to do mine own will, but the will of Him that sent me;"[286] and when He says, "Behold my mother and my brethren! For whosoever shall do the will of God,[287] the same is

---

283 *In excelsis*; Vulgate, *in altissimis*.

284 Luke ii. 14.

285 John iv. 34.

286 John vi. 38.

287 Vulgate, *Patris qui in cœlis* ("Father who is in heaven"). So the Greek.

my brother, and sister, and mother."[288] And therefore, in those at least who do the will of God, the will of God is accomplished; not because they cause God to will, but because they do what He wills, *i.e.* they do according to His will.

There is also that other interpretation, "Thy will be done as in heaven so on earth,"—as in the holy and just, so also in sinners. And this, besides, may be understood in two ways: either that we should pray even for our enemies (for what else are they to be reckoned, in spite of whose will the Christian and Catholic name still spreads?), so that it is said, "Thy will be done as in heaven so on earth,"—as if the meaning were, As the righteous do Thy will, in like manner let sinners also do it, so that they may be converted unto Thee; or in this sense, "Let Thy will be done as in heaven so on earth," so that every one may get his own; which will take place at the last judgment, the righteous being requited with a reward, sinners with condemnation—when the sheep shall be separated from the goats.[289]

That other interpretation also is not absurd, nay, it is thoroughly accordant with both our faith and hope,

---

288 Matt. xxii. 49, 50.
289 Matt. xxv. 33, 46.

that we are to take heaven and earth in the sense of spirit and flesh. And since the apostle says, "With the mind I myself serve the law of God, but with the flesh the law of sin,"[290] we see that the will of God is done in the mind, *i.e.* in the spirit. But when death shall have been swallowed up in victory, and this mortal shall have put on immortality, which will happen at the resurrection of the flesh, and at that change which is promised to the righteous, according to the prediction of the same apostle,[291] let the will of God be done on earth, as it is in heaven; *i.e.*, in such a way that, in like manner as the spirit does not resist God, but follows and does His will, so the body also may not resist the spirit or soul, which at present is harassed by the weakness of the body, and is prone to fleshly habit: and this will be an element of the perfect peace in the life eternal, that not only will the will be present with us, but also the performance of that which is good. "For to will," says he, "is present with me; but how to perform that which is good I find not:" for not yet in earth as in heaven, *i.e.* not yet in the flesh as in the spirit, is the will of God done. For even in our misery the will of God is done, when we suffer those things through the flesh

---

290 Rom. vii. 25.

291 1 Cor. xv. 42, 55.

which are due to us in virtue of our mortality, which our nature has deserved because of its sin. But we are to pray for this, that the will of God may be done as in heaven so in earth; that in like manner as with the heart we delight in the law after the inward man,[292] so also, when the change in our body has taken place, no part of us may, on account of earthly griefs or pleasures, stand opposed to this our delight.

Nor is that view inconsistent with truth, that we are to understand the words, "Thy will be done as in heaven so in earth," as in our Lord Jesus Christ Himself, so also in the Church: as if one were to say, As in the man who fulfilled the will of the Father, so also in the woman who is betrothed to him. For heaven and earth are suitably understood as if they were man and wife; since the earth is fruitful from the heaven fertilizing it.

---

292 Rom. vii. 18, 22.

Chapter VII

The fourth petition is, "Give us this day our daily bread." Daily bread is put either for all those things which meet the wants of this life, in reference to which He says in His teaching, "Take no thought for the morrow:" so that on this account there is added, "Give us this day:" or, it is put for the sacrament of the body of Christ, which we daily receive: or, for the spiritual food, of which the same Lord says, "Labour for the meat which perisheth not;"[293] and again, "I am the bread of life,[294] which came down from heaven."[295] But which of these three views is the more probable, is a question for consideration. For perhaps some one may wonder why we should pray that we may obtain the things which are necessary for this life,—such, for

---

[293] *Escam quæ non corrumpitur*; Vulgate, *non cibum qui perit.*
[294] *Panis vitæ*; Vulgate, *panis vivus.*
[295] John vi. 27, 41.

instance, as food and clothing,—when the Lord Himself says, "Be not anxious what ye shall eat, or what ye shall put on." Can any one not be anxious for a thing which he prays that he may obtain; when prayer is to be offered with so great earnestness of mind, that to this refers all that has been said about shutting our closets, and also the command, "Seek ye first the kingdom of God, and His righteousness; and all these things shall be added[296] unto you"? Certainly He does not say, Seek ye first the kingdom of God, and then seek those other things; but "all these things," says He, "shall be added unto you," that is to say, even though ye are not seeking them. But I know not whether it can be found out, how one is rightly said not to seek what he most earnestly pleads with God that he may receive.

But with respect to the sacrament of the Lord's body (in order that they may not start a question, who, the most of them being in Eastern parts, do not partake of the Lord's supper daily, while this bread is called daily bread: in order, therefore, that they may be silent, and not defend their way of thinking about this matter even by the very authority of the Church, because they do such things without scandal, and are

---

296 *Apponentur*; Vulgate, *adjicientur*.

not prevented from doing them by those who preside over their churches, and when they do not obey are not condemned; whence it is proved that this is not understood as daily bread in these parts: for, if this were the case, they would be charged with the commission of a great sin, who do not on that account receive it daily; but, as has been said, not to argue at all to any extent from the case of such parties), this consideration at least ought to occur to those who reflect, that we have received a rule for prayer from the Lord, which we ought not to transgress, either by adding or omitting anything. And since this is the case, who is there who would venture to say that we ought only once to use the Lord's Prayer, or at least that, even if we have used it a second or a third time before the hour at which we partake of the Lord's body, afterwards we are assuredly not so to pray during the remaining hours of the day? For we shall no longer be able to say, "Give us this day," respecting what we have already received; or every one will be able to compel us to celebrate that sacrament at the very last hour of the day.

It remains, therefore, that we should understand the daily bread as spiritual, that is to say, divine precepts, which we ought daily to meditate and to labour after. For just with respect to these the Lord

says, "Labour for the meat which perisheth not."
That food, moreover, is called daily food at present,
so long as this temporal life is measured off by means
of days that depart and return. And, in truth, so long
as the desire of the soul is directed by turns, now to
what is higher, now to what is lower, *i.e.* now to spiritual things, now to carnal, as is the case with him
who at one time is nourished with food, at another
time suffers hunger; bread is daily necessary, in order that the hungry man may be recruited, and he
who is falling down may be raised up. As, therefore,
our body in this life, that is to say, before that great
change, is recruited with food, because it feels loss;
so may the soul also, since by means of temporal
desires it sustains as it were a loss in its striving after
God, be reinvigorated by the food of the precepts.
Moreover, it is said, "Give us this day," as long as it
is called today, *i.e.* in this temporal life. For we shall
be so abundantly provided with spiritual food after
this life unto eternity, that it will not then be called
daily bread; because there the flight of time, which
causes days to succeed days, whence it may be called
today, will not exist. But as it is said, "Today, if ye

will hear His voice,"[297] which the apostle interprets in the Epistle to the Hebrews, As long as it is called today;[298] so here also the expression is to be understood, "Give us this day." But if any one wishes to understand the sentence before us also of food necessary for the body, or of the sacrament of the Lord's body, we must take all three meanings conjointly; that is to say, that we are to ask for all at once as daily bread, both the bread necessary for the body, and the visible hallowed bread, and the invisible bread of the word of God.[299]

---

[297] Ps. xcv. 7.

[298] Heb. iii. 13.

[299] The Greek ἐπιούσιος, translated *daily* (see margin of Revised Version, with alternate rendering of American Committee), is found only here and in Luke xi. 3. Its meaning does not seem to come under the review of Augustine, but has troubled modern commentators. It has been taken to mean (1) *needful*, hence sufficient, as opposed to superfluity or want (Chrysostom, Tholuck, Ewald, Ebrard, Weiss, etc.); (2) *daily* (Luther, English version, etc.); (3) *for the coming day* (Grotius, Meyer, Thayer, Lightfoot, who has an elaborate treatment in *Revision of English New Testament*, Append. pp. 195–245). The direct reference of the bread to spiritual food is given by the Vulgate, and generally accepted in the Roman Catholic Church. Olshausen, Delitzsch, Alford, etc., regard the spiritual nourishment involved by implication in the term.

Chapter VIII

The fifth petition follows: "And forgive us our debts, as we also forgive[300] our debtors." It is manifest that by debts are meant sins, either from that statement which the Lord Himself makes, "Thou shalt by no means come out thence, till thou hast paid the uttermost farthing;"[301] or from the fact that He called those men debtors who were reported to Him as having been killed, either those on whom the tower fell, or those whose blood Herod had mingled with the sacrifice. For He said that men supposed it was because they were debtors above measure, *i.e.* sinners, and added "I tell you, Nay: but, except ye repent, ye shall all likewise die."[302] Here, therefore,

---

300 The present with the Vulgate, *Textus Receptus, Teaching of Twelve Apostles.* The perfect is found in א, B, Z, etc., and adopted by Tischendorf, Westcott and Hort, and Revised Version.

301 Matt. v. 26.

302 Luke xiii. 1-5. *Moriemini*; Vulgate, *peribitis*. Augustine has written "Herod" instead of "Pilate."

it is not a money claim that one is pressed to remit, but whatever sins another may have committed against him. For we are enjoined to remit a money claim by that precept rather which has been given above, "If any man will sue thee at the law, and take away thy coat, let him have thy cloak also;"[303] nor is it necessary to remit a debt to every money debtor; but only to him who is unwilling to pay, to such an extent that he wishes even to go to law. "Now the servant of the Lord," as says the apostle, "must not go to law."[304] And therefore to him who shall be unwilling, either spontaneously or when requested, to pay the money which he owes, it is to be remitted. For his unwillingness to pay will arise from one of two causes, either that he has it not, or that he is avaricious and covetous of the property of another; and both of these belong to a state of poverty: for the former is poverty of substance, the latter poverty of disposition. Whoever, therefore, remits a debt to such an one, remits it to one who is poor, and performs a Christian work; while that rule remains in force, that he should be prepared in mind to lose what is owing to him. For if he has used exertion in every way, quietly and gently, to have it restored to him, not so much aiming at a money

303 Matt. v. 40.
304 2 Tim. ii. 24.

profit, as that he may bring the man round to what is right, to whom without doubt it is hurtful to have the means of paying, and yet not to pay; not only will he not sin, but he will even do a very great service, in trying to prevent that other, who is wishing to make gain of another's money, from making shipwreck of the faith; which is so much more serious a thing, that there is no comparison. And hence it is understood that in this fifth petition also, where we say, "Forgive us our debts," the words are spoken not indeed in reference to money, but in reference to all ways in which any one sins against us, and by consequence in reference to money also. For the man who refuses to pay you the money which he owes, when he has the means of doing so, sins against you. And if you do not forgive this sin, you will not be able to say, "Forgive us, as we also forgive;" but if you pardon it, you see how he who is enjoined to offer such a prayer is admonished also with respect to forgiving a money debt.

That may indeed be construed in this way, that when we say, "Forgive us our debts, as[305] we also forgive," then

---

305 Not "because," nor "to the same extent as," but "in the same manner as." It is interesting to note the contrast between the spirit of Christianity and Islam as indicated by a comparison of this petition with the prayer offered every night by the ten thousand students at the Mahometan college in Cairo: "I seek refuge with

only are we convicted of having acted contrary to this rule, if we do not forgive them who ask pardon, because we also wish to be forgiven by our most gracious Father when we ask His pardon. But, on the other hand, by that precept whereby we are enjoined to pray for our enemies, it is not for those who ask pardon that we are enjoined to pray. For those who are already in such a state of mind are no longer enemies. By no possibility, however, could one truthfully say that he prays for one whom he has not pardoned. And therefore we must confess that all sins which are committed against us are to be forgiven, if we wish those to be forgiven by our Father which we commit against Him. For the subject of revenge has been sufficiently discussed already, as I think.[306]

Allah from Satan the accursed. In the name of Allah the compassionate, the merciful, O Lord of all the creatures! O Allah! destroy the infidels and polytheists, thine enemies, the enemies of the religion. O Allah! make their children orphans, and defile their abodes. Cause their feet to slip," etc.

306 See Book i. chaps. 19, 20.

Chapter IX

The sixth petition is, "And bring[307] us not into temptation." Some manuscripts have the word "lead,"[308] which is, I judge, equivalent in meaning: for both translations have arisen from the one Greek word which is used. But many parties in prayer express themselves thus, "Suffer us not to be led into temptation;" that is to say, explaining in what sense the word "lead" is used. For God does not Himself lead, but suffers that man to be led into temptation whom He has deprived of His assistance, in accordance with a most hidden arrangement, and with his deserts. Often, also, for manifest reasons, He judges him worthy of being so deprived, and allowed to be led into temptation. But it is one thing to be led into temptation, another to be tempted. For without temptation no one can be

---

307 *Inferas…inducas*, as the Vulgate.
308 *Inferas…inducas*, as the Vulgate.

proved, whether to himself, as it is written, "He that
hath not been tempted, what manner of things doth
he know?"[309] or to another, as the apostle says, "And
your temptation in my flesh ye despised not:"[310] for
from this circumstance he learnt that they were stedfast, because they were not turned aside from charity by
those tribulations which had happened to the apostle
according to the flesh. For even before all temptations
we are known to God, who knows all things before
they happen.

When, therefore, it is said, "The Lord your God
tempteth (proveth) you, that He may know if ye love
Him,"[311] the words "that He may know" are employed
for what is the real state of the case, that He may make
you know: just as we speak of a joyful day, because it
makes us joyful; of a sluggish frost, because it makes us
sluggish; and of innumerable things of the same sort,
which are found either in ordinary speech, or in the
discourse of learned men, or in the Holy Scriptures.
And the heretics who are opposed to the Old Testament, not understanding this, think that the brand

---

309 Sir. xxxiv. 9, 11.
310 Gal. iv. 13, 14. The English version renders "*my* temptation,"
but "*your* temptation" is the reading of the oldest mss.
311 Deut. xiii. 3.

of ignorance, as it were, is to be placed upon Him of whom it is said, "The Lord your God tempteth you:" as if in the Gospel it were not written of the Lord, "And this He said to tempt (prove) him, for He Himself knew what He would do."[312] For if He knew the heart of him whom He was tempting, what is it that He wished to see by tempting him? But in reality, that was done in order that he who was tempted might become known to himself, and that he might condemn his own despair, on the multitudes being filled with the Lord's bread, while he had thought they had not enough to eat.

Here, therefore, the prayer is not, that we should not be tempted, but that we should not be brought into temptation: as if, were it necessary that any one should be examined by fire, he should pray, not that he should not be touched by the fire, but that he should not be consumed. For "the furnace proveth the potter's vessels, and the trial of tribulation righteous men."[313] Joseph therefore was tempted with the allurement of debauchery, but he was not brought into temptation.[314] Susanna was tempted, but she was not led or brought into

---

312 John vi. 6.

313 Ecclesiasticus xxvii. 5.

314 Gen. xxxix. 7-12.

temptation;[315] and many others of both sexes: but Job
most of all, in regard to whose admirable stedfastness
in the Lord his God, those heretical enemies of the Old
Testament, when they wish to mock at it with sacrile-
gious mouth, brandish this above other weapons, that
Satan begged that he should be tempted.[316] For they
put the question to unskilful men by no means able to
understand such things, how Satan could speak with
God: not understanding (for they cannot, inasmuch as
they are blinded by superstition and controversy) that
God does not occupy space by the mass of His corpo-
reity; and thus exist in one place, and not in another,
or at least have one part here, and another elsewhere:
but that He is everywhere present in His majesty, not
divided by parts, but everywhere complete. But if they
take a fleshly view of what is said, "The heaven is my
throne, and the earth is my footstool,"[317] —to which
passage our Lord also bears testimony, when He says,
"Swear not at all: neither by heaven, for it is God's
throne; nor by the earth, for it is His footstool,"[318]—
what wonder if the devil, being placed on earth, stood

---

315 Susanna i. 19-22.
316 Job i. 11.
317 Isa. lxvi. 1.
318 Matt. v. 34, 35.

before the feet of God, and spoke something in His presence? For when will they be able to understand that there is no soul, however wicked, which can yet reason in any way, in whose conscience God does not speak? For who but God has written the law of nature in the hearts of men?—that law concerning which the apostle says: "For when the Gentiles, which have not the law, do by nature the things contained in the law, these, having not the law, are a law unto themselves: which show the work of the law written in their hearts, their conscience also bearing them witness,[319] and their thoughts[320] the meanwhile accusing or else excusing one another, in the day when the Lord[321] shall judge the secrets of men."[322] And therefore, as in the case of every rational soul, which thinks and reasons, even though blinded by passion, we attribute whatever in its reasoning is true, not to itself but to the very light of truth by which, however faintly, it is according to its capacity illuminated, so as to perceive some measure of truth by its reasoning; what wonder if the

---

319 *Contestante*; Vulgate, *testimonium reddente.*

320 *Cogitationum accusantium*; Vulgate, *cogitationibus accusantibus.*

321 *Dominus*; Vulgate, *Deus.*

322 Rom. ii. 14-16.

depraved spirit of the devil, perverted though it be by lust, should be represented as having heard from the voice of God Himself, *i.e.* from the voice of the very Truth, whatever true thought it has entertained about a righteous man whom it was proposing to tempt? But whatever is false is to be attributed to that lust from which he has received the name of devil. Although it is also the case that God has often spoken by means of a corporeal and visible creature whether to good or bad, as being Lord and Governor of all, and Disposer according to the merits of every deed: as, for instance, by means of angels, who appeared also under the aspect of men; and by means of the prophets, saying, Thus saith the Lord. What wonder then, if, though not in mere thought, at least by means of some creature fitted for such a work, God is said to have spoken with the devil?

And let them not imagine it unworthy of His dignity, and as it were of His righteousness, that God spoke with him: inasmuch as He spoke with an angelic spirit, although one foolish and lustful, just as if He were speaking with a foolish and lustful human spirit. Or let such parties themselves tell us how He spoke with that rich man, whose most foolish covetousness He wished to censure, saying: "Thou fool, this night thy soul shall be required[323] of thee: then whose shall those things be which thou hast provided?"[324] Certainly the Lord Himself says so in the Gospel, to which those heretics, whether they will or no, bend their necks. But if they are puzzled by this circumstance, that Satan asks from God that a righteous man should be tempted; I do not explain how it happened, but I compel them to explain why it is said in the Gospel by the Lord Himself to the disciples, "Behold, Satan hath desired to have you, that he may sift you as wheat;"[325] and He says to Peter, "But I have prayed for thee, that thy faith fail not."[326] And when they explain this to me, they explain to themselves at the same time that which they question me about. But if they should not be able to explain this, let them not dare with rashness to blame in any book what they read in the Gospel without offence.

Temptations, therefore, take place by means of Satan not by his power, but by the Lord's permission, either for the purpose of punishing men for their sins, or of proving and exercising them in accordance with

---

323 *Anima expostulatur*; Vulgate, *animam repetunt.*

324 Luke xii. 20.

325 *Petit vos vexare quomodo triticum*; Vulgate, *expetivit vos ut cribraret sicut triticum.*

326 Luke xxii. 31, 32.

the Lord's compassion. And there is a very great difference in the nature of the temptations into which each
one may fall. For Judas, who sold his Lord, did not fall
into one of the same nature as Peter fell into, when,
under the influence of terror, he denied his Lord. There
are also temptations common to man, I believe, when
every one, though well disposed, yet yielding to human frailty, falls into error in some plan, or is irritated
against a brother, in the earnest endeavour to bring him
round to what is right, yet a little more than Christian
calmness demands: concerning which temptations the
apostle says, "There hath no temptation taken you but
such as is common to man;" while he says at the same
time, "But God is faithful, who will not suffer[327] you
to be tempted above that ye are able; but will with the
temptation also make a way to escape, that ye may be
able to bear[328] it."[329] And in that sentence he makes
it sufficiently evident that we are not to pray that we
may not be tempted, but that we may not be led into
temptation. For we are led into temptation, if such
temptations have happened to us as we are not able to
bear. But when dangerous temptations, into which it is

---

327 *Sinat*; Vulgate, *patietur*.

328 *Tolerare*; Vulgate, *sustinere*.

329 1 Cor. x. 13.

ruinous for us to be brought and led, arise either from prosperous or adverse temporal circumstances, no one is broken down by the irksomeness of adversity, who is not led captive by the delight of prosperity.[330]

The seventh and last petition is, "But deliver us from evil."[331] For we are to pray not only that we may not be led into the evil from which we are free, which is asked in the sixth place; but that we may also be delivered from that into which we have been already led. And when this has been done, nothing will remain terrible, nor will any temptation at all have to be feared. And yet in this life, so long as we carry about our present mortality, into which we were led by the persuasion of the serpent, it is not to be hoped that this can be the case; but yet we are to hope that at some future time it will take place: and this is the hope which is not seen, of which the apostle, when speaking, said, "But

---

330 Trench, giving the essence of Augustine's discussion, says, "God does tempt quite as truly as the devil tempts; all the difference lies in the end and aim with which they severally do it,—the one tempting to deceive, the other to approve: Satan, to their ruin; God, to their everlasting gain."

331 Alford and other modern commentators agree with Augustine in explaining ἀπὸ τοῦ πονηροῦ "of evil;" Bengel, Meyer, Schaff, and others (see Revised Version) make the form masculine,—"the Evil One."

hope which is seen is not hope."[332] But yet the wisdom which is granted in this life also, is not to be despaired of by the faithful servants of God. And it is this, that we should with the most wary vigilance shun what we have understood, from the Lord's revealing it, is to be shunned; and that we should with the most ardent love seek after what we have understood, from the Lord's revealing it, is to be sought after. For thus, after the remaining burden of this mortality has been laid down in the act of dying, there shall be perfected in every part of man at the fit time, the blessedness which has been begun in this life, and which we have from time to time strained every nerve to lay hold of and secure.

---

332 Rom. viii. 24.

Chapter X

But the distinction among these seven petitions is to be considered and commended. For inasmuch as our temporal life is being spent now, and that which is eternal hoped for, and inasmuch as eternal things are superior in point of dignity, albeit it is only when we have done with temporal things that we pass to the other; although the three first petitions begin to be answered in this life, which is being spent in the present world (for both the hallowing of God's name begins to be carried on just with the coming of the lord of humility; and the coming of His kingdom, to which He will come in splendour, will be manifested, not after the end of the world, but in the end of the world; and the perfect doing of His will in earth as in heaven, whether you understand by heaven and earth the righteous and sinners, or spirit and flesh, or the Lord and the Church, or all these things together, will be brought to completion just with the perfecting of our blessedness, and therefore at the close of the world), yet all three will remain to eternity. For both the hallowing of God's name will go on for ever, and there is no end of His kingdom, and eternal life is promised to our perfected blessedness. Hence those three things will remain consummated and thoroughly completed in that life which is promised us.

But the other four things which we ask seem to me to belong to this temporal life.[333] And the first of them is, "Give us this day our daily bread." For whether by this same thing which is called daily bread be meant spiritual bread, or that which is visible in the sacrament or in this sustenance of ours, it belongs to the present time, which He has called "today," not because spiritual food is not everlasting, but because that which is called daily food in the Scriptures is represented to the soul either by the sound of the expression or by temporal signs of any kind: things all of which will certainly no more have existence when all shall be taught of God,[334] and thus shall no longer be making known to others by movement of their bodies, but drinking

---

333 Or, as he expresses it in another place (*Sermon* lvii. 7), "to this life of our pilgrimage" ("*ista vita peregrinationis nostræ*").

334 Isa. liv. 13, John vi. 45.

in each one for himself by the purity of his mind the ineffable light of truth itself. For perhaps for this reason also it is called bread, not drink, because bread is converted into aliment by breaking and masticating it, just as the Scriptures feed the soul by being opened up and made the subject of discourse; but drink, when prepared, passes as it is into the body: so that at present the truth is bread, when it is called daily bread; but then it will be drink, when there will be no need of the labour of discussing and discoursing, as it were of breaking and masticating, but merely of drinking unmingled and transparent truth. And sins are at present forgiven us, and at present we forgive them; which is the second petition of these four that remain: but then there will be no pardon of sins, because there will be no sins. And temptations molest this temporal life; but they will have no existence when these words shall be fully realized, "Thou shall hide them in the secret of Thy presence."[335] And the evil from which we wish to be delivered, and the deliverance from evil itself, belong certainly to this life, which as being mortal we have deserved at the hand of God's justice, and from which we are delivered by His mercy.

---

335 Ps. xxxi. 20.

Chapter XI

The sevenfold number of these petitions also seems to me to correspond to that sevenfold number out of which the whole sermon before us has had its rise.[336] For if it is the fear of God through which the poor in spirit are blessed, inasmuch as theirs is the kingdom of heaven; let us ask that the name of God may be hallowed among men through that "fear which is clean, enduring for ever."[337] If it is piety through which the meek are blessed, inasmuch as they shall inherit the earth; let us ask that His kingdom may come, whether it be over ourselves, that we may become meek, and not resist Him, or whether it be from heaven to earth in the splendour of the Lord's advent, in which we shall rejoice, and shall be praised, when He says, "Come,

---

336 Lange draws a comparison between the petitions and the Beatitudes similar to that which follows.
337 Ps. xix. 9.

ye blessed of my Father, inherit[338] the kingdom prepared for you from the foundation[339] of the world."[340]
For "in the Lord," says the prophet, "shall my soul be
praised; the meek shall hear thereof, and be glad."[341] If
it is knowledge through which those who mourn are
blessed, inasmuch as they shall be comforted; let us
pray that His will may be done as in heaven so in earth,
because when the body, which is as it were the earth,
shall agree in a final and complete peace with the soul,
which is as it were heaven, we shall not mourn: for there
is no other mourning belonging to this present time,
except when these contend against each other, and
compel us to say, "I see another law in my members,
warring against the law of my mind;" and to testify our
grief with tearful voice, "O wretched[342] man that I am!
who shall deliver me from the body of this death?"[343]
If it is fortitude through which those are blessed who
hunger and thirst after righteousness, inasmuch as they
shall be filled; let us pray that our daily bread may be

---

338 *Accipite*; Vulgate, *possidete*.

339 *Origine*, Vulgate, *constitutione*.

340 Matt. xxv. 34.

341 Ps. xxxiv. 2.

342 *Miser*; Vulgate, *infelix*.

343 Rom. vii. 23, 24.

given to us today, by which, supported and sustained, we may be able to reach that most abundant fulness. If it is prudence through which the merciful are blessed, inasmuch as they shall obtain mercy; let us forgive their debts to our debtors, and let us pray that ours may be forgiven to us. If it is understanding through which the pure in heart are blessed, inasmuch as they shall see God; let us pray not to be led into temptation, lest we should have a double heart, in not seeking after a single good, to which we may refer all our actings, but at the same time pursuing things temporal and earthly. For temptations arising from those things which seem to men burdensome and calamitous, have no power over us, if those other temptations have no power which befall us through the enticements of such things as men count good and cause for rejoicing. If it is wisdom through which the peacemakers are blessed, inasmuch as they shall be called the children of God;[344] let us pray that we may be freed from evil, for that very freedom will make us free, *i.e.* sons of God, so that we may cry in the spirit of adoption, "Abba, Father."[345]

Nor are we indeed carelessly to pass by the circumstance, that of all those sentences in which the Lord has

344 Matt. v. 3-9.
345 Rom. viii. 15, Gal. iv. 6.

taught us to pray, He has judged that that one is chiefly to be commended which has reference to the forgiveness of sins: in which He would have us to be merciful, because it is the only wisdom for escaping misery. For in no other sentence do we pray in such a way that we, as it were, enter into a compact with God: for we say, "Forgive us, as we also forgive." And if we lie in that compact, the whole prayer is fruitless. For He speaks thus: "For if ye forgive men their trespasses, your heavenly Father will also forgive you: But if ye forgive not men their trespasses, neither will your Father forgive your trespasses."

CHAPTER XII

There follows a precept concerning fasting, having reference to that same purification of heart which is at present under discussion. For in this work also we must be on our guard, lest there should creep in a certain ostentation and hankering after the praise of man, which would make the heart double, and not allow it to be pure and single for apprehending God. "Moreover, when ye fast," says He, "be not, as the hypocrites, of a sad countenance: for they disfigure their faces,[346] that they may appear[347] unto men to fast. Verily I say unto you, they have their reward.

---

346 *Vultum...videantur*; Vulgate, *facies...appareant*. The Greek has a play on words, ἀφανίζουσι...φανῶσι ("they mar their appearance, that they may make an appearance").

347 *Vultum...videantur*; Vulgate, *facies...appareant*. The Greek has a play on words, ἀφανίζουσι...φανῶσι ("they mar their appearance, that they may make an appearance").

But ye,[348] when ye fast, anoint your head, and wash your face; that ye appear not unto men to fast, but unto your Father which is in secret: and your Father, which seeth in secret, shall reward you." It is manifest from these precepts that all our effort is to be directed towards inward joys, lest, seeking a reward from without, we should be conformed to this world, and should lose the promise of a blessedness so much the more solid and firm, as it is inward, in which God has chosen that we should become conformed to the image of His Son.[349]

But in this section it is chiefly to be noticed, that there may be ostentatious display not merely in the splendour and pomp of things pertaining to the booty, but also in doleful squalor itself; and the more dangerous on this account, that it deceives under the name of serving God. And therefore he who is very conspicuous

---

348 Vulgate has the singular as the Greek. The Pharisees were scrupulous in keeping fast-days. Monday and Thursday were observed by the strict with different degrees of scrupulosity,—the lowest admitting of washing and anointing the head. (See Schürer, *N. Zeitgesch.* p. 505 sqq.). The early practice of fasting in the sub-apostolic Church is evident from the *Teaching of the Twelve Apostles*, which enjoins it before baptism, and on the "fourth day and the Preparation Day" (vii., viii.).
349 Rom. viii. 29.

by immoderate attention to the body, and by the splendour of his clothing or other things, is easily convicted by the things themselves of being a follower of the pomps of the world, and misleads no one by a cunning semblance of sanctity; but in regard to him who under a profession of Christianity, fixes the eyes of men upon himself by unusual squalor and filth, when he does it voluntarily, and not under the pressure of necessity, it may be conjectured from the rest of his actings whether he does this from contempt of superfluous attention to the body, or from a certain ambition: for the Lord has enjoined us to beware of wolves under a sheep's skin; but "by their fruits," says He, "shall ye know them." For when by temptations of any kind those very things begin to be withdrawn from them or refused to them, which under that veil they either have obtained or desire to obtain, then of necessity it appears whether it is a wolf in a sheep's skin or a sheep in its own. For a Christian ought not to delight the eyes of men by superfluous ornament on this account, because pretenders also too often assume that frugal and merely necessary dress, that they may deceive those who are not on their guard: for those sheep also ought not to lay aside their own skins, if at any time wolves cover themselves there with.

It is usual, therefore, to ask what He means, when He says: "But ye, when ye fast, anoint your head, and wash your faces, that ye appear not unto men to fast." For it would not be right in any one to teach (although we may wash our face according to daily custom) that we ought also to have our heads anointed when we fast. If, then, all admit this to be most unseemly, we must understand this precept with respect to anointing the head and washing the face as referring to the inner man.[350] Hence, to anoint the head refers to joy; to wash the face, on the other hand, refers to purity: and therefore that man anoints his head who rejoices inwardly in his mind and reason. For we rightly understand that as being the head which has the preeminence in the soul, and by which it is evident that the other parts of man are ruled and governed. And this is done by him who does not seek his joy from without, so as to draw his delight in a fleshly way from the praises of men. For the flesh, which ought to be subject, is in no way the head of the whole nature of man. "No man," indeed, "ever yet hated his own flesh," as the apostle says, when giving the precept as to loving one's wife;[351] but the man is the head of the woman, and Christ is the head

---

350   So modern exegetes (Meyer, etc.).

351   Eph. v. 25-33.

of the man.[352] Let him, therefore, rejoice inwardly in
his fasting[353] in this very circumstance, that by his fasting he so turns away from the pleasure of the world as
to be subject to Christ, who according to this precept
desires to have the head anointed. For thus also he will
wash his face, *i.e.* cleanse his heart, with which he shall
see God, no veil being interposed on account of the
infirmity contracted from squalor; but being firm and
stedfast, inasmuch as he is pure and guileless. "Wash
you," says He, "make you clean; put away the evil of
your doings from before mine eyes."[354] From the squalor, therefore, by which the eye of God is offended, our
face is to be washed. For we, with open face beholding
as in a glass the glory of the Lord, are changed into the
same image.[355]

Often also the thought of things necessary belonging to this life wounds and defiles our inner eye; and
frequently it makes the heart double, so that in regard
to those things in which we seem to act rightly with
our fellow men, we do not act with that heart where-

---

[352] 1 Cor. xi. 3.

[353] "It hardly needs to add," says Trench, "that Augustine everywhere interprets *'when ye fast'* as a command."

[354] Isa. i. 16.

[355] 2 Cor. iii. 18.

with the Lord enjoins us; *i.e.*, it is not because we love them, but because we wish to obtain some advantage from them for the necessity of the present life. But we ought to do them good for their eternal salvation, not for our own temporal advantage. May God, therefore, incline our heart to His testimonies, and not to covetousness.[356] For "the end of the commandment is charity out of a pure heart, and of a good conscience, and of faith unfeigned."[357] But he who looks after his brother from a regard to his own necessities in this life, does not certainly do so from love, because he does not look after him whom he ought to love as himself, but after himself; or rather not even after himself, seeing that in this way he makes his own heart double, by which he is hindered from seeing God, in the vision of whom alone there is certain and lasting blessedness.

---

356 Ps. cxix. 36.
357 1 Tim. i. 5.

CHAPTER XIII

Rightly, therefore, does he who is intent on cleansing our heart follow up[358] what He has said with a precept, where He says: "Lay not up[359] for yourselves treasures upon earth, where moth and rust[360] doth corrupt,[361] and where thieves break through and steal: but lay up for yourselves treasures in heaven, where neither moth nor rust doth corrupt, and where thieves do not break through nor steal. For where your treasure is, there will your heart be[362] also." If, therefore, the heart be on earth, *i.e.* if one perform anything with a heart bent

---

358 Having uttered warnings against formalists, the Lord now passes to the complete dedication of the heart.

359 *Condere…tinea et comestura exterminant*; Vulgate, *thesaurizare… ærugo et tinea domolitur.*

360 Not the specific rust of metals; wider sense of *wear and tear.*

361 *Condere…tinea et comestura exterminant*; Vulgate, *thesaurizare… ærugo et tinea domolitur.*

362 *Erit*; Vulgate, *est.*

on obtaining earthly advantage, how will that heart be clean which wallows on earth? But if it be in heaven, it will be clean, because whatever things are heavenly are clean. For anything becomes polluted when it is mixed with a nature that is inferior, although not polluted of its kind; for gold is polluted even by pure silver, if it be mixed with it: so also our mind becomes polluted by the desire after earthly things, although the earth itself be pure of its kind and order. But we would not understand heaven in this passage as anything corporeal, because everything corporeal is to be reckoned as earth. For he who lays up treasure for himself in heaven ought to despise the whole world. Hence it is in that heaven of which it is said, "The heaven of heavens is the Lord's,[363] *i.e.* in the spiritual firmament: for it is not in that which is to pass away that we ought to fix and place our treasure and our heart, but in that which ever abideth; but heaven and earth shall pass away.[364]

And here He makes it manifest that He gives all these precepts with a view to the cleansing of the

---

363 Ps. cxv. 16.

364 Matt. xxiv. 35. Robert South gives his sermon on this passage the heading, "No man ever went to heaven whose heart was not there before." It has been remarked, as regards an earthly Church, one does not take abiding interest in it unless one gives toward it.

heart, when He says: "The candle[365] of the body is the eye: if therefore thine eye be single, thy whole body shall be full of light. But if thine eye be evil, thy whole body shall be full of darkness. If, therefore, the light [lamp][366] that is in thee be darkness, how great is that darkness!" And this passage we are to understand in such a way as to learn from it that all our works are pure and well-pleasing in the sight of God, when they are done with a single heart, *i.e.* with a heavenly intent, having that end of love in view; for love is also the fulfilling of the law.[367] Hence we ought to take the eye here in the sense of the intent itself, wherewith we do whatever we are doing; and if this be pure and right, and looking at that which ought to be looked at, all our works which we perform in accordance therewith are necessarily good. And all those works He has called the whole body; for the apostle also speaks of certain works of which he disapproves as our members, and teaches that they are to be mortified, saying, "Mortify therefore your members which are upon the

---

365 *Lucerna…lumen.*

366 *Lucerna…lumen.*

367 Rom. xiii. 10.

earth; fornication, uncleanness, covetousness,"[368] and all other such things.[369]

It is not, therefore, what one does, but the intent with which he does it, that is to be considered. For this is the light in us, because it is a thing manifest to ourselves that we do with a good intent what we are doing; for everything which is made manifest is light.[370] For the deeds themselves which go forth from us to human society, have an uncertain issue; and therefore He has called them darkness. For I do not know, when I present money to a poor man who asks it, either what he is to do with it, or what he is to suffer from it; and it may happen that he does some evil with it, or suffers some evil on account of it, a thing I did not wish to happen when I gave it to him, nor would I have given it with such an intention. If, therefore, I did it with a good intention,—a thing which was known to me when I was doing it, and is therefore called light,—my deed also is lighted up, whatever issue it shall have; but that issue, inasmuch as it is uncertain and unknown,

---

368 Col. iii. 5.

369 "Singleness of intention will preserve us from the snare of having a double treasure, and therefore a divided heart" (Plumptre).

370 Eph. v. 13. Augustine's rendering here is the true sense of the original.

is called darkness. But if I have done it with a bad intent, the light itself even is darkness. For it is spoken of as light, because every one knows with what intent he acts, even when he acts with a bad intent; but the light itself is darkness, because the aim is not directed singly to things above, but is turned downwards to things beneath, and makes, as it were, a shadow by means of a double heart. "If, therefore, the light that is in thee be darkness, how great is that darkness!" *i.e.*, if the very intent of the heart with which you do what you are doing (which is known to you) is polluted by the hunger after earthly and temporal things, and blinded, how much more is the deed itself, whose issue is uncertain, polluted and full of darkness! Because, although what you do with an intent which is neither upright nor pure, may turn out for some one's good, it is the way in which you have done it, not how it has turned out for him, that is reckoned to you.[371]

---

[371] The eye is as the *lamp* (Revised Version) through which the body gets light,—the organ whose proper work it is to transmit light. The blind have no light, because their lamp is out or destroyed. The light within us is "the reason, especially the practical reason" (Meyer); that which is left of the divine image in man (Tholuck); the reason that was left after the fall of Adam (Calvin); the Old Testament revelation perverted (Lange); the conscience (Alford). "The spirit of man is the candle (*lamp*, Revised Version)

of the Lord" (Prov. xx. 27): it guides the faculties of the soul. But
if it be in darkness how great is that darkness; *i.e.* the darkness
which already existed! What a terrible condition those are in who
do not receive the Spirit of enlightenment (who becomes the "inner light"), and feel no need of Him! "He whose affections are on
heavenly things, has his whole soul lighted; he whose affections
are depraved, has his understanding and his whole soul darkened
also" (Mansel).

CHAPTER XIV

Then, further, the statement which follows, "No man can serve two masters," is to be referred to this very intent, as He goes on to explain, saying: "For either he will hate the one, and love the other; or else he will[372] submit to the one, and despise the other." And these words are to be carefully considered; for who the two masters are he forthwith shows, when He says, "Ye cannot serve God and mammon." Riches are said to be called mammon among the Hebrews. The Punic name also corresponds: for gain is called mammon in Punic.[373] But he who serves mammon certainly serves him who, as being set over those earthly things in virtue of his perversity, is called by our Lord the prince of this

---

372 *Alterum patietur*; Vulgate, *unum sustinebit.*

373 Augustine is the only one to give this derivation. His residence in North Africa is the explanation of his knowledge of the Punic. The word probably comes from the Chaldee and through the Hebrew word *aman*, "what is trusted in." (See Thayer, *Lexicon.*)

world.[374] A man will therefore "either hate" this one, "and love the other," *i.e.* God; "or he will submit to the one, and despise the other." For whoever serves mammon submits to a hard and ruinous master: for, being entangled by his own lust, he becomes a subject of the devil, and he does not love him; for who is there who loves the devil? But yet he submits to him; as in any large house he who is connected with another man's maid servant submits to hard bondage on account of his passion. even though he does not love him whose maidservant he loves.

But "he will despise the other," He has said; not, he will hate. For almost no one's conscience can hate God; but he despises, *i.e.* he does not fear Him, as if feeling himself secure in consideration of His goodness. From this carelessness and ruinous security the Holy Spirit recalls us, when He says by the prophet, "My son, do not add sin upon sin, and say, The mercy of God is great ;"[375] and, "Knowest thou not that the patience[376] of God inviteth[377] thee to repentance?"[378] For whose

---

374 John xii. 31, John xiv. 30.

375 Sir. v. 5, 6.

376 *Patientia…invitat*; Vulgate, *benignitas…adducit.*

377 *Patientia…invitat*; Vulgate, *benignitas…adducit.*

378 Rom. ii. 4.

mercy can be mentioned as being so great as His, who pardons all the sins of those who return, and makes the wild olive a partaker of the fatness of the olive? and whose severity as being so great as His, who spared not the natural branches, but broke them off because of unbelief?[379] But let not any one who wishes to love God, and to beware of offending Him, suppose that he can serve two masters;[380] and let him disentangle the upright intention of his heart from all doubleness: for thus he will think of the Lord with a good heart, and in simplicity of heart will seek Him.[381]

---

379 Rom. xi. 17-24.

380 Luther says the world can do it in a masterly way, and carry the tree (or "water" according to the English figure) on both shoulders. This verse is a rebuke to those who think they can combine a supreme affection for heavenly and for earthly things at the same time, and pursue both with equal zeal.

381 Wisdom i. 1.

Chapter XV

"Therefore," says He, "I say unto you, Have not anxiety[382] for your life, what ye shall eat;[383] nor yet for your body, what ye shall put on." Lest perchance, although it is not now superfluities that are sought after, the heart should be made double by reason of necessaries themselves, and the aim should be wrenched aside to seek after those things of our own, when we are doing something as it were from compassion; *i.e.* so that when we wish to appear to be consulting for some one's good, we are in that matter looking after our own profit rather than his advantage: and we do not seem to ourselves to be sinning for this reason, that it is not superfluities, but necessaries, which we wish to obtain. But the Lord admonishes us that we should remember that God, when He made and compounded us of body

---

382 *Habere sollicitudinem*; Vulgate, *sollicitæ sitis.*
383 *Edatis*; Vulgate, *manducetis.*

and soul, gave us much more than food and clothing, through care for which He would not have us make our hearts double. "Is not," says He, "the soul more than the meat?" So that you are to understand that He who gave the soul will much more easily give meat. "And the body than the raiment," *i.e.* is more than raiment: so that similarly you are to understand, that He who gave the body will much more easily give raiment.

And in this passage the question is wont to be raised, whether the food spoken of has reference to the soul, since the soul is incorporeal, and the food in question is corporeal food. But let us admit that the soul in this passage stands for the present life, whose support is that corporeal nourishment. In accordance with this signification we have also that statement: "He that loveth his soul shall lose it."[384] And here, unless we understand the expression of this present life, which we ought to lose for the kingdom of God, as it is clear the martyrs were able to do, this precept will be in contradiction to that sentence where it is said: "What is a man profited, if he shall gain the whole world, and lose[385] his own soul?"[386]

---

384 John xii. 25.

385 *Detrimentum faciat*; Vulgate, *detrimentum patiatur*.

386 Matt. xvi. 26.

"Behold," says He, "the fowls of the air: for they sow not, neither do they reap, nor gather into barns; yet your heavenly Father feedeth them: are ye not much better than they?" *i.e.* ye are of more value. For surely a rational being such as man has a higher rank in the nature of things than irrational ones, such as birds. "Which of you, by taking thought,[387] can add one cubit unto his stature?[388] And why take ye thought for raiment?" That is to say, the providence of Him by whose power and sovereignty it has come about that your body was brought up to its present stature, can also clothe you; but that it is not by your care that it has come about that your body should arrive at this stature, may be understood from this circumstance, that if you should take thought, and should wish to add one cubit to this stature, you cannot. Leave, therefore, the care of

---

387 *Curans*; Vulgate, *cogitans*.

388 The term ἡλικία, translated by Augustine and the Vulgate *statura*, and by the English version *stature*, more probably means the *measure of life*, or *age* (American notes to Revised Version, Tholuck, De Wette, Trench, Alford, Meyer, Schaff, Plumptre, Weiss, etc.) A cubit was equal to the length of the forearm. The force of the Lord's words would be greatly diminished if such a measure was conceived of as possible to be added to the stature. The idea is, that human ingenuity and labor cannot add the least measure.

protecting the body to Him by whose care you see it has come about that you have a body of such a stature.

But an example was to be given for the clothing too, just as one is given for the food. Hence He goes on to say, "Consider the lilies of the field, how they grow; they toil not, neither do they spin: and yet I say unto you, that even Solomon[389] in all his glory was not arrayed[390] like one of these. Wherefore, if God so clothe the grass of the field, which today is, and tomorrow is cast into the oven; shall He not much more clothe you, O ye of little faith?" But these examples are not to be treated as allegories, so that we should inquire what the fowls of heaven or the lilies of the field mean: for they stand here, in order that from smaller matters we may be persuaded respecting greater ones;[391] just as is the case in regard to the judge who neither feared God nor regarded man, and yet yielded to the widow who often importuned him to consider her case, not from piety

---

389 To the Jew the highest representative of splendour and pomp.

390 *Vestitutus*; Vulgate, *coopertus*. "As the beauties of the flower are unfolded by the divine Creator Spirit from *within*, from the laws and capacities of its own individual life, so must all true adornment of man be unfolded from *within* by the same Spirit. This hidden meaning must not be overlooked" (Alford). The law of spiritual growth is mysterious and spontaneous.

391 The argument, so called, *a minore ad majus*.

or humanity, but that he might be saved annoyance. For that unjust judge does not in any way allegorically represent the person of God; but yet as to how far God, who is good and just, cares for those who supplicate Him, our Lord wished the inference to be drawn from this circumstance, that not even an unjust man can despise those who assail him with unceasing petitions, even were his motive merely to avoid annoyance.[392]

---

392 Luke xviii. 2-8.

CHAPTER XVI

"Therefore be not anxious," says He," saying, What shall we eat?[393] or, What shall we drink? or, Wherewithal shall we be clothed?[394] (For after all these things do the Gentiles seek:) for your Father knoweth that ye have need of all these things. But seek ye first the kingdom of God and His righteousness; and all these things shall be added[395] unto you." Here He shows most manifestly that these things are not to be sought as if they were our blessings in such sort, that on account of them we ought to do well in all our actings, but yet that they are necessary. For what the difference is between a blessing which is to be sought, and a necessary which is to be taken for use, He has made plain by this sentence, when He says, "Seek ye first the

---

393 *Edemus…vestiemur*; Vulgate, *manducabimus…operiemur.*

394 *Edemus…vestiemur*; Vulgate, *manducabimus…operiemur.*

395 *Apponentur*; Vulgate, *adjicientur.*

kingdom of God and His righteousness, and all these things shall be added unto you."[396] The kingdom and the righteousness of God therefore are our good; and this is to be sought, and there the end is to be set up, on account of which we are to do everything which we do. But because we serve as soldiers in this life, in order that we may be able to reach that kingdom, and because our life cannot be spent without these necessaries, "These things shall be added unto you," says He; "but seek ye first the kingdom of God and His righteousness." For in using that word "first," He has indicated that this is to be sought later, not in point of time, but in point of importance: the one as being our good, the other as being something necessary for us; but the necessary on account of that good.

For neither ought we, for example, to preach the gospel with this object, that we may eat; but to eat with this object, that we may preach the gospel: for if we preach the gospel for this cause, that we may eat, we reckon the gospel of less value than food; and in that case our good will be in eating, but that which is necessary for us in preaching the gospel. And this the apostle also forbids, when he says it is lawful for

---

396 Matt. vi. 33.

himself even, and permitted by the Lord, that they who preach the gospel should live of the gospel, *i.e.* should have from the gospel the necessaries of this life; but yet that he has not made use of this power. For there were many who were desirous of having an occasion for getting and selling the gospel, from whom the apostle wished to cut off this occasion, and therefore he submitted to a way of living by his own hands.[397] For concerning these parties he says in another passage, "That I may cut off occasion from them which seek[398] occasion."[399] Although even if, like the rest of the good apostles, by the permission of the Lord he should live of the gospel, he would not on that account place the end of preaching the gospel in that living, but would rather make the gospel the end of his living; *i.e.*, as I have said above, he would not preach the gospel with this object, that he might get his food and all other necessaries; but he would take such things for this purpose, in order that he might carry out that other object, viz. that willingly, and not of necessity, he should preach the gospel. For this he disapproves of when he says, "Do ye not know, that

---

397 Acts xx. 34.

398 *Quærunt*; Vulgate, *volunt.*

399 2 Cor. xi. 12.

they which minister in the temple[400] eat the things
which are of the temple? and they which wait at the
altar are partakers with the altar? Even so hath the
Lord ordained that they which preach the gospel
should live of the gospel. But I have used none of
these things." Hence he shows that it was permitted,
not commanded; otherwise he will be held to have
acted contrary to the precept of the Lord. Then he
goes on to say: "Neither have I written these things,
that it should be so done unto me: for it were better
for me to die, than that any man should make my glo-
rying void."[401] This he said, as he had already resolved,
because of some who were seeking occasion, to gain a
living by his own hands. "For if I preach the gospel,"
says he, "I have nothing to glory of:" *i.e.*, if I preach
the gospel in order that such things may be done in
my case, or, if I preach with this object, in order that
I may obtain those things, and if I thus place the end
of the gospel in meat and drink and clothing. But
wherefore has he nothing to glory of? "Necessity," says
he," is laid upon me;" *i.e.* so that I should preach the
gospel for this reason, because I have not the means of
living, or so that I should acquire temporal fruit from

---

400 *Templo*; Vulgate, *sacrario*.
401 *Inanem faciat*; Vulgate, *evacuet*.

the preaching of eternal things; for thus, consequently, the preaching of the gospel will be a matter of necessity, not of free choice. "For woe is unto me," says he, "if I preach not the gospel!" But how ought he to preach the gospel? Evidently in such a way as to place the reward in the gospel itself, and in the kingdom of God: for thus he can preach the gospel, not of constraint, but willingly. "For if I do this thing willingly," says he, "I have a reward: but if against my will, a dispensation of the gospel is committed unto me;"[402] if, constrained by the want of those things which are necessary for temporal life, I preach the gospel, others will have through me the reward of the gospel, who love the gospel itself when I preach it; but I shall not have it, because it is not the gospel itself I love, but its price lying in those temporal things. And this is something sinful, that any one should minister the gospel not as a son, but as a servant to whom a stewardship of it has been committed; that he should, as it were, pay out what belongs to another, but should himself receive nothing from it except victuals, which are given not in consideration of his sharing in the kingdom, but from without, for the support of a mis-

---

402 1 Cor. ix. 13-17.

erable bondage. Although in another passage he calls himself also a steward. For a servant also, when adopted into the number of the children, is able faithfully to dispense to those who share with him that property in which he has acquired the lot of a fellow-heir. But in the present case, where he says, "But if against my will, a dispensation (stewardship) is committed unto me," he wished such a steward to be understood as dispenses what belongs to another, and from it gets nothing himself.

Hence anything whatever that is sought for the sake of something else, is doubtless inferior to that for the sake of which it is sought; and therefore that is first for the sake of which you seek such a thing, not the thing which you seek for the sake of that other. And for this reason, if we seek the gospel and the kingdom of God for the sake of food, we place food first, and the kingdom of God last; so that if food were not to fail us, we would not seek the kingdom of God: this is to seek food first, and then the kingdom of God. But if we seek food for this end, that we may gain the kingdom of God, we do what is said, "Seek ye first the kingdom of God and His righteousness; and all these things shall be added unto you."[403]

---

[403] Nor is it said, "Seek…in *order that* all these things may be added:" simply, "*and all*," etc., yet largely inclusive,—sanctity *and* comfort. The comfort follows naturally. The passage is a rebuke to those who condemn the amenities of life and art, and a caution to those who place these things before themselves as a chief end. The passage justifies the statement that religion (or godliness) is profitable for the life that now is. The Psalmist never saw the *righteous* forsaken. A traditional saying of Jesus, quoted by Clement, Origen, and Eusebius, runs, "Ask great things, and little things shall be added; ask heavenly things, and earthly things shall be added."

CHAPTER XVII

For in the case of those who are seeking first the kingdom of God and His righteousness, *i.e.* who are preferring this to all other things, so that for its sake they are seeking the other things, there ought not to remain behind the anxiety lest those things should fail which are necessary to this life for the sake of the kingdom of God. For He has said above, "Your Father knoweth that ye have need of all these things." And therefore, when He had said, "Seek ye first the kingdom of God and His righteousness," He did not say, Then seek such things (although they are necessary), but He affirms "all these things shall be added unto you,"[404] *i.e.* will follow, if ye

---

404 Nor is it said, "Seek…in *order that* all these things may be added:" simply, *"and all,"* etc., yet largely inclusive,—sanctity *and* comfort. The comfort follows naturally. The passage is a rebuke to those who condemn the amenities of life and art, and a caution to those who place these things before themselves as a chief end. The passage justifies the statement that religion (or godliness) is profitable for

seek the former, without any hindrance on your part: lest while ye seek such things, ye should be turned away from the other; or lest ye should set up two things to be aimed at, so as to seek both the kingdom of God for its own sake, and such necessaries: but these rather for the sake of that other; so shall they not be wanting to you. For ye cannot serve two masters. But the man is attempting to serve two masters, who seeks both the kingdom of God as a great good, and these temporal things. He will not, however, be able to have a single eye, and to serve the Lord God alone, unless he take all other things, so far as they are necessary, for the sake of this one thing, *i.e.* for the sake of the kingdom of God. But as all who serve as soldiers receive provisions and pay, so all who preach the gospel receive food and clothing. But all do not serve as soldiers for the welfare of the republic, but some do so for what they get: so also all do not minister to God for the welfare of the Church, but some do so for the sake of these temporal things, which they are to obtain in the shape as it were of provisions and pay; or both for the one thing and for the other. But it has been already

---

the life that now is. The Psalmist never saw the *righteous* forsaken. A traditional saying of Jesus, quoted by Clement, Origen, and Eusebius, runs, "Ask great things, and little things shall be added; ask heavenly things, and earthly things shall be added."

said above, "Ye cannot serve two masters." Hence it is with a single heart and only for the sake of the kingdom of God that we ought to do good to all; and we ought not in doing so to think either of the temporal reward alone, or of that along with the kingdom of God: all which temporal things He has placed under the category of tomorrow, saying, "Take no thought for tomorrow."[405] For tomorrow is not spoken of except in time, where the future succeeds the past. Therefore, when we do anything good, let us not think of what is temporal, but of what is eternal; then will that be a good and perfect work. "For the morrow," says He, "will be anxious for the things of itself;"[406] *i.e.*, so that, when you ought, you will take food, or drink, or clothing, that is to say, when necessity itself begins to urge you. For these things will be within reach, because our Father knoweth that we have need of all these things. For "sufficient unto the

---

[405] *Cogitare in crastino*; Vulgate, *solliciti esse in crastinum*. There is no uniformity in Augustine's or the Vulgate's translation of the Greek μεριμνάω ("take anxious thought") in this passage.

[406] The morrow will bring its own vexations and anxieties. The English version entirely misleads as to the meaning of the special clause, "will take care of itself." The Revised Version is a literal translation, and at least gives the true sense by implication. But with each day's temptations and troubles, it is implied, special enablement and deliverance will be provided.

day," says He, "is the evil thereof;"[407] *i.e.* it is sufficient
that necessity itself will urge us to take such things. And
for this reason, I suppose, it is called evil, because for
us it is penal: for it belongs to this frailty and mortality
which we have earned by sinning. Do not add, therefore,
to this punishment of temporal necessity anything more
burdensome, so that you should not only suffer the want
of such things, but should also for the purpose of satisfy-
ing this want enlist as a soldier for God.

In the use of this passage, however, we must be very
specially on our guard, lest perchance, when we see any
servant of God making provision that such necessaries
shall not be wanting either to himself or to those with
whose care he has been entrusted, we should decide
that he is acting contrary to the Lord's precept, and is
anxious for the morrow.[408] For the Lord Himself also,

407 Wiclif, following the Vulgate, translates *malice*; Tyndale, *trou-
ble*; the Genevan Bible, *grief*.
408 Our Lord's precept is not against provident forethought,—of
which Augustine goes on to give examples,—but against anxious
thought which implies distrust of God's providence. Anxious, fret-
ful, distrustful care for the future, unreliant upon God's bounty,
wisdom, and love (as implied in the address, *your heavenly Father*)
is declared to be unnecessary (25, 26), foolish (27–30), and hea-
thenish (32, "After these things do the Gentiles seek"). The passages teach trust in God, who is more interested in His children than
in the fowls of the air, and will certainly take care of them.

although angels ministered to Him,[409] yet for the sake of example, that no one might afterwards be scandalized when he observed any of His servants procuring such necessaries, condescended to have money bags, out of which whatever might be required for necessary uses might be provided; of which bags, as it is written, Judas, who betrayed Him, was the keeper and the thief.[410] In like manner, the Apostle Paul also may seem to have taken thought for the morrow, when he said: "Now concerning the collection for the saints, as I have given order to the saints of Galatia, even so do ye: upon the first day of the week let every one of you lay by him in store[411] what shall seem good unto him, that there be no gatherings when I come. And when I come[412] whomsoever ye shall approve by your letters, them will I send to bring your liberality unto Jerusalem. And if it be meet that I go also, they shall go with me. Now I will come unto you when I shall pass through Macedonia: for I shall pass through Macedonia. And it may be that I will abide, yea, and winter with you, that ye may bring me on my journey whithersoever I go. For I

---

409 Matt. iv. 11.

410 John xii. 6.

411 *Thesaurizans*; Vulgate, *recondens*.

412 *Advenero*; Vulgate, *præsens fuero*.

will not see you now by the way; but I trust to tarry a while with you, if the Lord permit. But I will tarry at Ephesus until Pentecost."[413] In the Acts of the Apostles also it is written, that such things as are necessary for food were provided for the future, on account of an impending famine. For we thus read: "And in these days came prophets down from Jerusalem to Antioch,[414] and there was great rejoicing. And when we were gathered together,[415] there stood up one of them named Agabus, and signified by the Spirit that there should be great dearth throughout all the world: which came to pass in the days of Claudius Cæsar. Then the disciples, every one according to his ability, determined to send relief to the elders for the brethren which dwelt in Judæa, which also they did by the hands of Barnabas and Saul."[416] And in the case of the necessaries presented to him, wherewith the same Apostle Paul when setting sail was laden,[417] food seems to have been furnished

---

413 1 Cor. xvi. 1-8.

414 Not in the original Greek or Vulgate, but implied in the preceding context.

415 Not in the original Greek or Vulgate, but implied in the preceding context.

416 Acts xi. 27-30. The clause shows much divergence from the Vulgate in construction.

417 Acts xxviii. 10.

for more than a single day. And when the same apostle writes, "Let him that stole steal no more: but rather let him labour, working[418] with his hands the thing which is good, that he may have to give to him that needeth;"[419] to those who misunderstand him he does not seem to keep the Lord's precept, which runs, "Behold the fowls of the air; for they sow not, neither do they reap, nor gather into barns;" and, "Consider the lilies of the field, how they grow; they toil not, neither do they spin;" while he enjoins the parties in question to labour, working with their hands, that they may have something which they may be able to give to others also. And in what he often says of himself, that he wrought with his hands that he might not be burdensome;[420] and in what is written of him, that he joined himself to Aquila on account of the similarity of their occupation, in order that they might work together at that from which they might make a living;[421] he does not seem to have imitated the birds of the air and the lilies of the field. From these and such like passages of

---

418 *Operans*; Vulgate, *operando*.

419 Eph. iv. 28. *Unde tribuere cui opus est*; Vulgate, *unde tribuat necessitatem patienti*.

420 1 Thess. ii. 9, 2 Thess. iii. 8.

421 Acts xviii. 2, 3.

Scripture, it is sufficiently apparent that our Lord does not disapprove of it, when one looks after such things in the ordinary way that men do; but only when one enlists as a soldier of God for the sake of such things, so that in what he does he fixes his eye not on the kingdom of God, but on the acquisition of such things.

Hence this whole precept is reduced to the following rule, that even in looking after such things we should think of the kingdom of God, but in the service of the kingdom of God we should not think of such things. For in this way, although they should sometimes be wanting (a thing which God often permits for the purpose of exercising us), they not only do not weaken our proposition, but even strengthen it, when it is examined and tested. For, says He, "we glory in tribulations also; knowing that tribulation worketh patience, and patience experience, and experience hope: And hope maketh not ashamed, because the love of God is shed abroad in our hearts by the Holy Ghost which is given unto us."[422] Now, in the mention of his tribulations and labours, the same apostle mentions that he has had to endure not only prisons and shipwrecks and many such like annoyances, but also

---

422 Rom. v. 3-5.

hunger and thirst, cold and nakedness.[423] But when we read this, let us not imagine that the promises of God have wavered, so that the apostle suffered hunger and thirst and nakedness while seeking the kingdom and righteousness of God, although it is said to us, "Seek ye first the kingdom of God and His righteousness; and all these things shall be added unto you:" since that Physician to whom we have once for all entrusted ourselves wholly, and from whom we have the promise of life present and future, knows such things just as helps, when He sets them before us, when He takes them away, just as He judges it expedient for us; whom He rules and directs as parties who require both to be comforted and exercised in this life, and after this life to be established and confirmed in perpetual rest. For man also, when he frequently takes away the fodder from his beast of burden, is not depriving it of his care, but rather does what he is doing in the exercise of care.

---

[423] 2 Cor. xi. 23-27.

Chapter XVIII

A nd inasmuch as when such things are either provided against the time to come, or reserved, if
there is no cause wherefore you should expend them, it
is uncertain with what intention it is done, since it may
be done with a single heart, and also with a double one,
He has seasonably added in this passage: "Judge not,[424]
that ye be not judged.[425] For with what judgment ye
judge, ye shall be judged,[426] and with what measure ye
mete, it shall be measured to you again." In this passage, I am of opinion that we are taught nothing else,
but that in the case of those actions respecting which it

---

[424] *Sine scientia, amore, necessitate* ("without knowledge, love,
necessity."—Bengel). The discussion is one of the most thorough
and satisfactory sections of Augustine's commentary.

[425] *Judicetur de vobis...judicabitur*; Vulgate, *judicemini...judica-
bimini*.

[426] *Judicetur de vobis...judicabitur*; Vulgate, *judicemini...judica-
bimini*.

is doubtful with what intention they are done, we are to put the better construction on them. For when it is written, "By their fruits ye shall know them," the statement has reference to things which manifestly cannot be done with a good intention; such as debaucheries, or blasphemies, or thefts, or drunkenness, and all such things, of which we are permitted to judge, according to the apostle's statement: "For what have I to do to judge them also that are without? do not ye judge them that are within?"[427] But concerning the kind of food, because every kind of human food can be taken indiscriminately with a good intention and a single heart, without the vice of concupiscence, the same apostle forbids that they who ate flesh and drank wine be judged by those who abstained from such kinds of sustenance: "Let not him that eateth," says he, "despise him that eateth not; and let not him which eateth not, judge him that eateth." There also he says: "Who art thou that judges another man's servant? to his own master he standeth or falleth."[428] For in reference to such matters as can be done with a good and single and noble intention, although they may also be done with an intention the reverse of good, those parties wished, howbeit they

---

427 1 Cor. v. 12.
428 Rom. xiv. 3, 4.

were [mere] men, to pronounce judgment upon the secrets of the heart, of which God alone is Judge.

To this category belongs also what he says in another passage: "Therefore judge nothing before the time, until the Lord come, who both will bring to light the hidden things of darkness, and will make manifest the thoughts[429] of the hearts: and then shall every man have praise of God."[430] There are therefore certain ambiguous actions, respecting which we are ignorant with what intention they are performed, because they may be done both with a good or with an evil one, of which it is rash to judge, especially for the purpose of condemning. Now the time will come for these to be judged, when the Lord "will bring to light the hidden things of darkness, and will make manifest the counsels of the hearts." In another passage also the same apostle says: "Some men's aims are manifest beforehand, going before to judgment; and some men they follow after." He calls those sins manifest, with regard to which it is clear with what intention they are done; these go before to judgment, because if a judgment shall follow, it is not rash. But those which are concealed follow, because neither shall they remain hid in their own time. So we

---

429 *Cogitationes*; Vulgate, *consilia.*
430 1 Cor. iv. 5.

must understand with respect to good works also. For he adds to this effect: "Likewise also the good works of some are manifest beforehand; and they that are otherwise cannot be hid."[431] Let us judge, therefore, with respect to those which are manifest; but respecting those which are concealed, let us leave the judgment to God: for they also cannot be hid, whether they be good or evil, when the time shall come for them to be manifested.

There are two things, moreover, in which we ought to beware of rash judgment; when it is uncertain with what intention anything is done; or when it is uncertain what sort of a person he is going to be, who at preset is manifestly either good or bad. If, therefore, any one, for example, complaining of his stomach, would not fast, and you, not believing this, were to attribute it to the vice of gluttony, you would judge rashly. Likewise, if you were to come to know the gluttony and drunkenness as being manifest, and were so to administer reproof as if the man could never be amended and changed, you would nevertheless judge rashly. Let us not therefore reprove those things about which we do not know with what intention they are done; nor let

---

431 1 Tim. v. 24, 25.

us so reprove those things which are manifest, as that we should despair of a return to a right state of mind; and thus we shall avoid the judgment of which in the present instance it is said, "Judge not, that ye be not judged."

But what He says may cause perplexity: "For with what judgment ye judge, ye shall be judged; and with what measure ye mete, it shall be measured to you again." Is it the case, then, that if we shall judge anything with a rash judgment, God will also judge rashly with respect to us? or if we shall measure anything with an unjust measure, is there with God also an unjust measure, according to which it shall be measured to us again? (for by the expression measure also, I suppose the judgment itself is meant.) By no means does God either judge rashly, or recompense to anyone with an unjust measure; but it is so expressed, inasmuch as that very same rashness wherewith you punish another must necessarily punish yourself. Unless, perchance, it is to be imagined that injustice does harm in some way to him against whom it goes forth, but in no way to him from whom it goes forth; but nay, it often does no harm to him who suffers the injury, but it must necessarily do harm to him who inflicts it. For what harm did the injustice of the persecutors do to the martyrs?

None; but very much to the persecutors themselves. For although some of them were turned from the error of their ways, yet at the time at which they were acting as persecutors, their wickedness was blinding them. So also a rash judgment frequently does no harm to him who is the object of the rash judgment; but to him who judges rashly, the rashness itself must necessarily do harm. According to such a rule, I judge of that saying also: "Every one that strikes[432] with the sword shall perish with the sword."[433] For how many take the sword, and yet do not perish with the sword, Peter himself being an instance! But lest any should think that he escaped such punishment by the pardon of his sins (although nothing could be more absurd than to think that the punishment of the sword, which did not befall Peter, could have been greater than that of the cross, which actually befell him), yet what would they say of the malefactors who were crucified with our Lord; for both he who got pardon, got it after he was crucified, and the other did not get it at all?[434] Or had they perhaps crucified all whom they had slain; and did they therefore themselves too deserve to suffer the

---

432 *Omnis qui percusserit*; Vulgate, *omnes qui acceperint.*

433 Matt. xxvi. 52.

434 Luke xxiii. 33-43.

same thing? It is ridiculous to think so. For what else is meant by the statement, "For all they that take the sword shall perish with the sword," but that the soul dies by that very sin, whatever it may be, which it has committed?

Chapter XIX

And inasmuch as the Lord is admonishing us in this passage with respect to rash and unjust judgment,—for He wishes that whatever we do, we should do it with a heart that is single and directed toward God alone; and inasmuch as, with respect to many things, it is uncertain with what intention they are done, regarding which it is rash to judge; inasmuch, moreover, as those parties especially judge rashly respecting things that are uncertain, and readily find fault, who love rather to censure and to condemn than to amend and to improve, which is a fault arising either from pride or from envy; therefore He has subjoined the statement: "And why beholdest thou the mote that is in thy brother's eye, but considerest not the beam that is in thine own eye?" So that if perchance, for example, he has transgressed in anger, you should find fault in hatred; there being, as it were, as much difference between anger and hatred as between a mote and a beam. For hatred is inveterate anger, which, as it were simply by its long duration, has acquired so great strength as to be justly called a beam. Now, it may happen that, though you are angry with a man, you wish him to be turned from his error; but if you hate a man, you cannot wish to convert him.

"Or how wilt[435] thou say to thy brother, Let me pull out the mote out of thine eye; and, behold, a beam is in thine own eye? Thou hypocrite, first cast out the beam out of thine own eye; and then shalt thou see clearly to cast out the mote out of thy brother's eye;" *i.e.*, first cast the hatred away from thee, and then, but not before, shalt thou be able to amend him whom thou lovest.[436] And He well says, "Thou hypocrite." For to make complaint against vices is the duty of good and benevolent men; and when bad men do it, they are acting a part which does not belong to them; just like hypocrites, who conceal under a mask what they are,

---

435 The meaning is, how wilt thou have the effrontery to say, dare to say. The precept forbids all meddling, censoriousness, and captious faultfinding, and the spirit of slander, backbiting, calumny, etc.

436 "Ere you remark another's sin, Bid your own conscience look within." —Cowper.

and show themselves off in a mask what they are not. Under the designation hypocrites, therefore, you are to understand pretenders. And there is, in fact, a class of pretenders much to be guarded against, and troublesome, who, while they take up complaints against all kinds of faults from hatred and spite, also wish to appear counsellors. And therefore we must piously and cautiously watch, so that when necessity shall compel us to find fault with or rebuke any one, we may reflect first whether the fault is such as we have never had, or one from which we have now become free; and if we have never had it, let us reflect that we are men, and might have had it; but if we have had it, and are now free from it, let the common infirmity touch the memory, that not hatred but pity may go before that fault-finding or administering of rebuke: so that whether it shall serve for the conversion of him on whose account we do it, or for his perversion (for the issue is uncertain), we at least from the singleness of our eye may be free from care. If, however, on reflection, we find ourselves involved in the same fault as he is whom we were preparing to censure, let us not censure nor rebuke; but yet let us mourn deeply over the case, and let us invite him not to obey us, but to join us in a common effort.

For in regard also to what the apostle says,—"Unto the Jews I became as a Jew, that I might gain the Jews; to them that are under the law, as under the law (not being under the law), that I might gain them that are under the law; to them that are without law, as without law (being not without law to God, but under the law to Christ), that I might gain them that are without law. To the weak became I as weak, that I might gain the weak: I am made all things to all men, that I might gain all,"—he did not certainly so act in the way of pretence, as some wish it to be understood, in order that their detestable pretence may be fortified by the authority of so great an example; but he did so from love, under the influence of which he thought of the infirmity of him whom he wished to help as if it were his own. For this he also lays as the foundation beforehand, when he says: "For although I be free from all men, yet have I made myself servant unto all, that I might gain[437] the more."[438] And that you may understand this as being done not in pretence, but in love, under the influence of which we have compassion for men who are weak as if we were they, he thus admonishes us in another passage, saying, "Brethren, ye have been called unto

437 *Lucrifacerem*; Vulgate, *facerem salvos*.
438 1 Cor. ix. 19-22.

liberty; only use not liberty for an occasion to the flesh, but by love serve one another."[439] And this cannot be done, unless each one reckon the infirmity of another as his own, so as to bear it with equanimity, until the party for whose welfare he is solicitous is freed from it.

Rarely, therefore, and in a case of great necessity, are rebukes to be administered; yet in such a way that even in these very rebukes we may make it our earnest endeavour, not that we, but that God, should be served. For He, and none else, is the end: so that we are to do nothing with a double heart, removing from our own eye the beam of envy, or malice, or pretence, in order that we may see to cast the mote out of a brother's eye. For we shall see it with the dove's eyes,—such eyes as are declared to belong to the spouse of Christ,[440] whom God hath chosen for Himself a glorious Church, not having spot or wrinkle,[441] *i.e.* pure and guileless.

---

439 Gal. v. 13.

440 Song of Sol. iv. 1.

441 Eph. v. 27.

Chapter XX

But inasmuch as the word "guileless" may mislead some who are desirous of obeying God's precepts, so that they may think it wrong, at times, to conceal the truth, just as it is wrong at times to speak a falsehood, and inasmuch as in this way,—by disclosing things which the parties to whom they are disclosed are unable to bear,—they may do more harm than if they were to conceal them altogether and always, He very rightly adds: "Give not that which is holy to the dogs, neither cast ye your pearls before swine, lest they trample them under their feet, and turn again and rend you." For the Lord Himself, although He never told a lie, yet showed that He was concealing certain truths, when He said, "I have yet many things to say unto you, but ye cannot bear them now."[442] And the Apostle Paul, too, says: "And I, brethren, could not speak unto you

---

442 John xvi. 12.

as unto spiritual, but as unto carnal, even as unto babes
in Christ. I have fed you with milk, and not with meat:
for hitherto ye were not able to bear it, neither yet now
are ye able. For ye are yet carnal."[443]

Now, in this precept by which we are forbidden
to give what is holy to the dogs, and to cast our pearls
before swine, we must carefully require what is meant
by holy, what by pearls, what by dogs, what by swine.
A holy thing is something which it is impious to vi-
olate and to corrupt; and the very attempt and wish
to commit that crime is held to be criminal, although
that holy thing should remain in its nature inviolable
and incorruptible. By pearls, again, are meant whatever spiritual things we ought to set a high value upon,
both because they lie hid in a secret place, are as it were
brought up out of the deep, and are found in wrap-
pings of allegory, as it were in shells that have been
opened. We may therefore legitimately understand that
one and the same thing may be called both holy and a
pearl: but it gets the name of holy for this reason, that
it ought not to be corrupted; of a pearl for this reason,
that it ought not to be despised. Every one, however,
endeavours to corrupt what he does not wish to remain

---

443 1 Cor. iii. 1, 2.

uninjured: but he despises what he thinks worthless, and reckons to be as it were beneath himself; and therefore whatever is despised is said to be trampled on. And hence, inasmuch as dogs spring at a thing in order to tear it in pieces, and do not allow what they are tearing in pieces to remain in its original condition, "Give not," says He, "that which is holy unto the dogs:" for although it cannot be torn in pieces and corrupted, and remains unharmed and inviolable, yet we must think of what is the wish of those parties who bitterly and in a most unfriendly spirit resist, and, as far as in them lies, endeavour, if it were possible, to destroy the truth. But swine, although they do not, like dogs, fall upon an object with their teeth, yet by recklessly trampling on it defile it: "Do not *therefore* cast your pearls before swine, lest they trample them under their feet, and turn again and rend you." We may therefore not unsuitably understand dogs as used to designate the assailants of the truth, swine the despisers of it.

But when He says, "they turn again and rend you," He does not say, they rend the pearls themselves. For by trampling on them, just when they turn in order that they may hear something more, they yet rend him by whom the pearls have just been cast before them which they have trampled on. For you would not easily find out what pleasure the man could have who has trampled pearls under foot, *i.e.* has despised divine things whose discovery is the result of great labour. But in regard to him who teaches such parties, I do not see how he would escape being rent in pieces through their anger and wrathfulness. Moreover, both animals are unclean, the dog as well as the swine. We must therefore be on our guard, lest anything should be opened up to him who does not receive it: for it is better that he should seek for what is hidden, than that he should either attack or slight at what is open. Neither, in fact, is any other cause found why they do not receive those things which are manifest and of importance, except hatred and contempt, the one of which gets them the name of dogs, the other that of swine. And all this impurity is generated by the love of temporal things, *i.e.* by the love of this world, which we are commanded to renounce, in order that we may be able to be pure. The man, therefore, who desires to have a pure and single heart, ought not to appear to himself blameworthy, if he conceals anything from him who is unable to receive it. Nor is it to be supposed from this that it is allowable to lie: for it does not follow that when truth is concealed, falsehood is uttered. Hence, steps are to be taken first, that the hindrances which prevent his receiving it may be removed; for certainly if pollution is the reason he does not receive it, he is to be cleansed either by word or by deed, as far as we can possibly do it.

Then, further, when our Lord is found to have made certain statements which many who were present did not accept, but either resisted or despised, He is not to be thought to have given that which is holy to the dogs, or to have cast pearls before swine: for He did not give such things to those who were not able to receive them, but to those who were able, and were at the same time present; whom it was not meet that He should neglect on account of the impurity of others. And when tempters put questions to Him, and He answered them, so that they might have nothing to gainsay, although they might pine away from the effects of their own poisons, rather than be filled with His food, yet others, who were able to receive His teaching, heard to their profit many things in consequence of the opportunity created by these parties. I have said this, lest anyone, perhaps, when he is not able to reply to one who puts a question to him, should seem to himself excused, if he should say that he is unwilling to give that which is holy to the dogs, or to cast pearls before swine. For he who knows what to answer ought to do it, even for the sake of others, in whose minds despair arises, if they believe

that the question proposed cannot be answered: and
this in reference to matters that are useful, and that
belong to saving instruction. For many things which
may be the subject of inquiry on the part of idle people are needless and vain, and often hurtful, respecting
which, however, something must be said; but this very
point is to be opened up and explained, viz. why such
things ought not to form the subject of inquiry. In reference, therefore, to things that are useful, we ought
sometimes to give a reply to what is asked of us: just
as the Lord did, when the Sadducees had asked Him
about the woman who had seven husbands, to which
of them she would belong in the resurrection. For He
answered that in the resurrection they will neither marry, nor be given in marriage, but will be as the angels
in heaven. But sometimes, he who asks is to be asked
something else, by telling which he would answer himself as to the matter he asked about; but if he should
refuse to make a statement, it would not seem to those
who are present unfair, if he himself should not hear
anything as to the matter he inquired about. For those
who put the question, tempting Him, whether tribute
was to be paid, were asked another question, viz. whose
image the money bore which was brought forward by
themselves; and because they told what they had been

asked, *i.e.* that the money bore the image of Cæsar, they gave a kind of answer to themselves in reference to the question they had asked the Lord: and accordingly from their answer He drew this inference, "Render therefore unto Cæsar the things which are Cæsar's, and unto God the things that are God's."[444] When, however, the chief priests and elders of the people had asked by what authority He was doing those things, He asked them about the baptism of John: and when they would not make a statement which they saw to be against themselves, and yet would not venture to say anything bad about John, on account of the bystanders, "Neither tell I you," says He, "by what authority I do these things;"[445] a refusal which appeared most just to the bystanders. For they said they were ignorant of that which they really knew, but did not wish to tell. And, in truth, it was right that they who wished to have an answer to what they asked, should themselves first do what they required to be done toward them; and if they had done this, they would certainly have answered themselves. For they themselves had sent to John, asking who he was; or rather they themselves, being priests and Levites, had been sent, supposing that he was the

---

444 Matt. xxii. 15-34.
445 Matt. xxi. 23-27.

very Christ, but he said that he was not, and gave forth a testimony concerning the Lord:[446] a testimony respecting which if they chose to make a confession, they would teach themselves by what authority as the Christ He was doing those things; which as if ignorant of they had asked, in order that they might find an avenue for calumny.

---

446 John i. 19-27.

Chapter XXI

Since, therefore, a command had been given that what is holy should not be given to dogs, and pearls should not be cast before swine, a hearer might object and say, conscious of his own ignorance and weakness, and hearing a command addressed to him, that he should not give what he felt that he himself had not yet received,—might (I say) object and say, What holy thing do you forbid me to give to the dogs, and what pearls do you forbid me to cast before swine, while as yet I do not see that I possess such things? Most opportunely He has added the statement: "Ask, and it shall be given you; seek, and ye shall find; knock, and it shall be opened unto you. For every one that asketh receiveth; and he that seeketh findeth; and to him that knocketh it shall be opened." The asking refers to the obtaining by request soundness and strength of mind, so that we may be able to discharge those duties which are commanded; the seeking, on the other hand, refers to the finding of the truth. For inasmuch as the blessed life is summed up in action and knowledge, action wishes for itself a supply of strength, contemplation desiderates that matters should be made clear: of these therefore the first is to be asked, the second is to be sought; so that the one may be given, the other found. But knowledge in this life belongs rather to the way than to the possession itself: but whoever has found the true way, will arrive at the possession itself which, however, is opened to him that knocks.

In order, therefore, that these three things—viz. asking, seeking, knocking—may be made clear, let us suppose, for example, the case of one weak in his limbs, who cannot walk: in the first place, he is to be healed and strengthened so as to be able to walk; and to this refers the expression He has used, "Ask." But what advantage is it that he is now able to walk, or even run, if he should go astray by devious paths? A second thing therefore is, that he should find the road that leads to the place at which he wishes to arrive; and when he has kept that road, and arrived at the very place where he wishes to dwell, if he find it closed, it will be of no use either that he has been able to walk, or that he has walked and arrived, unless it be opened to him; to this, therefore, the expression refers which has been used, "Knock."

Moreover, great hope has been given, and is given, by Him who does not deceive when He promises: for He says, "Every one that asketh, receiveth; and he that seeketh, findeth; and to him that knocketh, it shall be opened." Hence there is need of perseverance, in order that we may receive what we ask, and find what we seek, and that what we knock at may be opened.[447] Now, just as He talked of the fowls of heaven and of the lilies of the field, that we might not despair of food and clothing being provided for us, so that our hopes might rise from lesser things to greater; so also in this passage, "Or what man is there of you," says He, "whom if his son ask bread, will he give him a stone? Or if he ask a fish, will he give him a serpent? If ye then, being evil, know how to give good gifts unto your children, how much more shall your Father which is in heaven give good things to them that ask Him?" How do the evil give good things? Now, He has called those evil[448] who

---

[447] The conditions of effective prayer are, that it should be made in the name of Christ (John xv. 16), with faith, and according to God's will (1 John v. 14).

[448] This has been regarded as a strong proof text for the doctrine of original sin. Bengel calls it "a shining testimony for original

are as yet the lovers of this world and sinners. And, in fact, the good things are to be called good according to their feeling, because they reckon these to be good things. Although in the nature of things also such things are good, but temporal, and pertaining to this feeble life: and whoever that is evil gives them, does not give of his own; for the earth is the Lord's, and the fulness thereof,[449] who made heaven, and earth, the sea, and all that therein is.[450] How much reason, therefore, there is for the hope that God will give us good things when we ask Him, and that we cannot be deceived, so that we should get one thing instead of another, when we ask Him; since we even, although we are evil, know how to give that for which we are asked? For we do not deceive our children; and whatever good things we give are not given of our own, but of what is His.

---

sin." Stier says it is "the strongest proof text for original sin in the whole of the Holy Scriptures." Meyer says the reference is to actual sin; while Plumptre declares that "the words at once recognise the fact of man's depravity, and assert that it is not total."

449 Ps. xxiv. 1.
450 Ps. cxlvi. 6.

Chapter XXII

Moreover, a certain strength and vigour in walking along the path of wisdom ties in good morals, which are made to extend as far as to purification and singleness of heart,—a subject on which He has now been speaking long, and thus concludes: "Therefore all good[451] things whatsoever ye would that men should do to you, do ye even so to them: for this is the law and the prophets." In the Greek copies we find the passage runs thus: "Therefore all things whatsoever ye would that men should do to you, do ye even so to them." But I think the word "good" has been added by the Latins to make the sentence clear. For the thought occurred, that if any one should wish something wicked to be done to him, and should refer this clause to that,— as, for instance, if one should wish to be challenged to drink immoderately, and to get drunk over his cups,

---

451 *Bona*; the Vulgate does not contain it.

and should first do this to the party by whom he wishes it to be done to himself,—it would be ridiculous to imagine that he had fulfilled this clause. Inasmuch, therefore, as they were influenced by this consideration, as I suppose, one word was added to make the matter clear; so that in the statement, "Therefore all things whatsoever ye would that men should do to you," there was inserted the word "good." But if this is wanting in the Greek copies, they also ought to be corrected: but who would venture to do this? It is to be understood, therefore, that the clause is complete and altogether perfect, even if this word be not added. For the expression used, "whatsoever ye would," ought to be understood as used not in a customary and random, but in a strict sense. For there is no will except in the good: for in the case of bad and wicked deeds, desire is strictly spoken of, not will. Not that the Scriptures always speak in a strict sense; but where it is necessary, they so keep a word to its perfectly strict meaning, that they do not allow anything else to be understood.

Moreover, this precept seems to refer to the love of our neighbour, and not to the love of God also, seeing that in another passage He says that there are two precepts on which "hang all the law and the prophets." For if He had said, All things whatsoever ye would should

be done to you, do ye even so; in this one sentence
He would have embraced both those precepts: for it
would soon be said that every one wishes that he himself should be loved both by God and by men; and
so, when this precept was given to him, that what he
wished done to himself he should himself do, that certainly would be equivalent to the precept that he should
love God and men. But when it is said more expressly
of men, "Therefore all things whatsoever ye would that
men should do to you, do ye even so to them," nothing else seems to be meant than, "Thou shalt love thy
neighbour as thyself."[452] But we must carefully attend
to what He has added here: "for this is the law and the
prophets." Now, in the case of these two precepts, He
not merely says, The law and the prophets hang; but

---

[452] The nearest approach that any uninspired Jewish teacher
came to the Golden Rule—the designation by which these words
are known—was the saying of Hillel, "What is unpleasant to thyself, do not to thy neighbour. This is the whole law, and all the
rest is commentary upon it." Beautiful as the saying is, it falls behind Christ's words, because it is merely negative, while they are a
positive requirement. The Stoics and the Chinese ethics also have
a similar negative precept. It is strange that the *Teaching of the
Twelve Apostles* (i. 2) gives the negative form, and not the positive
precept. Augustine says we ought to be glad when writers before
Christ spoke things in the Gospel (*En. in Ps.* cxl. 6).

He has also added, "all the law and the prophets,"[453] which is the same as the whole of prophecy: and in not making the same addition here, He has kept a place for the other precept, which refers to the love of God. Here, then, inasmuch as He is following out the precepts with respect to a single heart, and it is to be dreaded lest any one should have a double heart toward those from whom the heart can be hid, *i.e.* toward men, a precept with respect to that very thing was to be given. For there is almost nobody that would wish that any one of double heart should have dealings with himself. But no one can bestow anything upon a fellow man with a single heart, unless he so bestow it that he expects no temporal advantage from him, and does it with the intention which we have sufficiently discussed above, when we were speaking of the single eye.

The eye, therefore, being cleansed and rendered single, will be adapted and suited to behold and contemplate its own inner light. For the eye in question is the eye of the heart. Now, such an eye is possessed by him who, in order that his works may be truly good, does not make it the aim of his good works that he should please men; but even if it should turn out that

---

453 Matt. xxii. 37-40.

he pleases them, he makes this tend rather to their salvation and to the glory of God, not to his own empty boasting; nor does he do anything that is good tending to his neighbour's salvation for the purpose of gaining by it those things that are necessary for getting through this present life; nor does he rashly condemn a man's intention and wish in that action in which it is not apparent with what intention and wish it has been done; and whatever kindnesses he shows to a man, he shows them with the same intention with which he wishes them shown to himself, viz. as not expecting any temporal advantage from him: thus will the heart be single and pure in which God is sought. "Blessed," therefore, "are the pure in heart: for they shall see God."[454]

---

454 Matt. v. 8.

Chapter XXIII

B ut because this belongs to few, He now begins
to speak of searching for and possessing wisdom,
which is a tree of life; and certainly, in searching
for and possessing, *i.e.* contemplating this wisdom,
such an eye is led through all that precedes to a point
where there may now be seen the narrow way and
the strait gate. When, therefore, He says in continu-
ation, "Enter ye[455] in at the strait gate: for wide is the
gate, and broad is the way, that leadeth to destruction, and many there be which go in thereat: because
strait is the gate, and narrow is the way, which leadeth
unto life, and few there be that find it;[456] He does not

---

455 *Introite*; Vulgate, *intrate*.

456 The narrowness of the way is taken to represent the self-
denial and hardships of disciples (Meyer, Mansel, etc.), or righteousness (Bengel, Schaff, etc.). "The picture is a dark one, and
yet it represents but too faithfully the impression made, I do not
say on Calvinist or true Christian, but on any ethical teacher,

say so for this reason, that the Lord's yoke is rough, or His burden heavy; but because few are willing to bring their labours to an end, giving too little credit to Him who cries, "Come unto me, all ye that labour, and I will give you rest. Take my yoke upon you, and learn of me; for I am meek and lowly in heart: for my yoke is easy,[457] and my burden[458] is light"[459] (hence, moreover, the sermon before us took as its starting point the lowly and meek in heart): and this easy yoke and light burden which many spurn, few submit to; and on that account the way becomes narrow which leadeth unto life, and the gate strait by which it is entered.

by the actual state of mankind around us. If there is any wider hope, it is found in hints and suggestions of the possibilities of the future (1 Pet. iii. 19, 1 Pet. iv. 6)," etc. (Plumptre).

457 *Lene...sarcina*; Vulgate, *suave...onus.*
458 *Lene...sarcina*; Vulgate, *suave...onus.*
459 Matt. xi. 28-30.

Chapter XXIV

Here, therefore, those who promise a wisdom and a knowledge of the truth which they do not possess, are especially to be guarded against; as, for instance, heretics, who frequently commend themselves on account of their fewness. And hence, when He had said that there are few who find the strait gate and the narrow way, lest they [the heretics] should falsely substitute themselves under the pretext of their fewness, He immediately added, "Beware of false prophets,[460] which come to you in sheep's clothing, but inwardly they are ravening wolves." But such parties do not deceive the single eye, which knows how to distinguish a tree by its fruits. For He says: "Ye shall know them by their fruits." Then He adds the similitudes: "Do men gather grapes of thorns, or figs of thistles? Even so, every good tree bringeth forth good fruit; but a corrupt tree

---

[460] *Cavete a pseudoprophetis*; Vulgate, *attendite a falsis prophetis.*

bringeth forth evil fruit. A good tree cannot bring forth evil fruit, neither can a corrupt tree bring forth good fruit. Every tree that bringeth not forth good fruit[461] is hewn down, and cast into the fire. Wherefore by their fruits ye shall know them."

And in [the interpretation of] this passage we must be very much on our guard against the error of those who judge from these same two trees that there are two original natures, the one of which belongs to God, but the other neither belongs to God nor springs from Him. And this error has both been already discussed in other books [of ours][462] very copiously, and if that is still too little, will be discussed again; but at present we have merely to show that the two trees before us do not help them. In the first place, because it is so clear that He is speaking of men, that whoever reads what goes before and what follows will wonder at their blindness. Secondly, they fix their attention on

---

461 Excellency of fruitage is sanctity of life (*Bonitas fructuum est sanctitas vitæ* (Bengel).

462 More particularly his works against the Manichæans, *Contra Faustum Manichæum*, etc. Augustine also made much use of this passage against the Pelagians, to show that the will must be aided to produce good thoughts and deeds; that the unregenerate man is incapable of restoring himself.

what is said, "A good tree cannot bring forth evil fruit, neither can a corrupt tree bring forth good fruit," and therefore think that neither can it happen that an evil soul should be changed into something better, nor a good one into something worse; as if it were said, A good tree cannot become evil, nor an evil tree good. But it is said, "A good tree cannot bring forth evil fruit, neither can a corrupt tree bring forth good fruit." For the tree is certainly the soul itself, *i.e.* the man himself, but the fruits are the works of the man; an evil man, therefore, cannot perform good works, nor a good man evil works. If an evil man, therefore, wishes to perform good works, let him first become good. So the Lord Himself says in another passage more plainly: "Either make the tree good, or make the tree bad." But if He were figuratively representing the two natures of such parties by these two trees, He would not say, "Make:" for who of the sons of men can make a nature? Then also in that passage, when He had made mention of these two trees, He added, "Ye hypocrites, how can ye, being evil, speak good things?"[463] As long, therefore, as any one is evil, he cannot bring forth good fruits; for if he were to bring forth good fruits, he would no longer

---

463 Matt. xii. 33, 34.

be evil. So it might most truly have been said, snow cannot be warm; for when it begins to be warm, we no longer call it snow, but water. It may therefore come about, that what was snow is no longer so; but it cannot happen that snow should be warm. So it may come about, that he who was evil is no longer evil; it cannot, however, happen that an evil man should do good. And although he is sometimes useful, this is not the man's own doing; but it is done through him, in virtue of the arrangements of divine providence: as, for instance, it is said of the Pharisees, "What they bid you, do; but what they do, do not consent to do." This very circumstance, that they spoke things that were good, and that the things which they spoke were usefully listened to and done, was not a matter belonging to them: for, says He, "they sit in Moses' seat."[464] It was, therefore, when engaged through divine providence in preaching the law of God, that they were able to be useful to their hearers, although they were not so to themselves. Respecting such it is said in another place by the prophet, "They have sown wheat, but shall reap thorns;"[465] because they teach what is good, and do what is evil. Those, therefore, who listened to them, and did what

---

464 Matt. xxiii. 3, 2.
465 Jer. xii. 13.

was said by them, did not gather grapes of thorns, but through the thorns gathered grapes of the vine: just as, were any one to thrust his hand through a hedge, or were at least to gather a grape from a vine which was entangled in a hedge, that would not be the fruit of the thorns, but of the vine.

The question, indeed, is most rightly put, What are the fruits He would wish us to attend to, whereby we might know the tree? For many reckon among the fruits certain things which belong to the sheep's clothing, and in this way are deceived by wolves: as, for instance, either fastings, or prayers, or almsgivings; but unless all of these things could be done even by hypocrites, He would not say above, "Take heed that ye do not your righteousness before men, to be seen of them." And after prefixing this sentence, He goes on to speak of those very three things, almsgiving, prayer, fasting. For many give largely to the poor, not from compassion, but from vanity; and many pray, or rather seem to pray, while not keeping God in view, but desiring to please men; and many fast, and make a wonderful show of abstinence before those to whom such things appear difficult, and by whom they are reckoned worthy of honour: and catch them with artifices of this sort, while they hold up to view one thing for the purpose of deceiving, and put forth another for the purpose of preying upon or killing those who cannot see the wolves under that sheep's clothing. These, therefore, are not the fruits by which He admonishes us that the tree is known. For such things, when they are done with a good intention in sincerity, are the appropriate clothing of sheep; but when they are done in wicked deception, they cover nothing else but wolves. But the sheep ought not on this account to hate their own clothing, because the wolves often conceal themselves therein.

What the fruits are by the finding of which we may know an evil tree, the apostle tells us: "Now the works of the flesh are manifest, which are these; adulteries, fornications, uncleanness, lasciviousness, idolatry, witchcraft, hatreds, variances, emulations, wrath, strife, seditions, heresies, envyings, murders, drunkenness, revellings, and such like: of the which I tell you before, as I have also told you in time past, that they which do such things shall not inherit the kingdom of God." And what the fruits are by which we may know a good tree, the very same apostle goes on to tell us: "But the fruit of the Spirit is love, joy, peace, long-suffering, gentleness, goodness, faith, meekness, temperance."[466] It must be known, indeed, that "joy" stands here in a strict and proper sense; for bad men are, strictly speaking, not said to rejoice, but to make extravagant demonstrations of joy: just as we have said above, that "will" which the wicked do not possess, stands in a strict sense where it is said, "All things whatsoever ye would that men should do to you, do ye even so to them." In accordance with that strict sense of the word, in virtue of which joy is spoken of only in the good, the prophet also speaks, saying: "Rejoicing is not for the wicked, saith the Lord."[467] So also "faith" stands, not certainly as meaning any kind of it, but true faith: and the other things which find a place here have certain resemblances of their own in bad men and deceivers; so that they entirely mislead, unless one has the pure and single eye by which he may know such things. It is accordingly the best arrangement, that the cleansing of the eye is first discussed, and then mention is made of what things were to be guarded against.

---

[466] Gal. v. 19-23.

[467] Isa. lvii. 21, according to the Septuagint.

Chapter XXV

But seeing that, however pure an eye one may have, *i.e.* with however single and sincere a heart one may live, he yet cannot look into the heart of another: whatever things could not have become apparent in deeds or words, are disclosed by trials. Now trial is twofold; either in the hope of obtaining some temporal advantage, or in the terror of losing it. And especially must we be on our guard, lest, when striving after wisdom, which can be found in Christ alone, in whom are hid all the treasures of wisdom and knowledge;[468] —we must be on our guard, I say, lest, under the very name of Christ, we be deceived by heretics, or by any parties whatever defective in intelligence, and lovers of this world. For on this account He adds a warning, saying, "Not every one that saith unto Me, Lord, Lord,[469] shall

---

[468] Col. ii. 3.

[469] Many called Him Lord, but He never called any one Lord

enter into the kingdom of heaven; but he that doeth the will of My Father which is in heaven, he shall enter into the kingdom of heaven:" lest we should think that the mere fact of one saying to our Lord, "Lord, Lord," belongs to those fruits; and from that he should seem to us to be a good tree. But those are the fruits, to do the will of the Father who is in heaven, in the doing of which He has condescended to exhibit Himself as an example.

But the question may fairly be started, how with this sentence the statement of the apostle is to be reconciled, where he says, "No man speaking by the Spirit of God calleth Jesus accursed; and no man can say that Jesus is the Lord, but by the Holy Ghost:"[470] for neither can we say that any who have the Holy Spirit will not enter into the kingdom of heaven, if they persevere onwards to the end; nor can we affirm that those who say, "Lord, Lord," and yet do not enter into the kingdom of heaven, have the Holy Spirit. How then does no one say "that Jesus is the Lord, but by the Holy Ghost," unless it is because the apostle has used the word "say" here in a strict and proper sense, so that it implies the

---

(*ipsum multi, etiam amplissimi viri,—ipse neminem ne Pilatum quidem*, dominum *vocavit*.—Bengel).

[470] 1 Cor. xii. 3.

will and understanding of him who says? But the Lord
has used the word which He employs in a general sense:
"Not every one that saith unto Me, Lord, Lord, shall
enter into the kingdom of heaven." For he also who
neither wishes nor understands what he says, seems to
say it; but he properly says it, who gives expression to
his will and mind by the sound of his voice: just as, a
little before, what is called "joy" among the fruits of
the Spirit is called so in a strict and proper sense, not in
the way in which the same apostle elsewhere uses the
expression, "Rejoiceth not in iniquity:"[471] as if any one
could rejoice in iniquity: for that transport of a mind
making confused and boisterous demonstrations of joy
is not joy; for this latter is possessed by the good alone.
Hence those also seem to say it, who neither perceive
with the understanding nor engage with the deliberate
consent of the will in this which they utter, but utter it
with the voice merely; and after this manner the Lord
says, "Not every one that saith unto Me, Lord, Lord,
shall enter into the kingdom of heaven." But truly and
properly those parties say it whose utterance in speech
really represents their will and intention; and it is in
accordance with this signification that the apostle has

---

471 1 Cor. xiii. 6.

said, "No one can say that Jesus is the Lord, but by the Holy Ghost."

And besides, it belongs especially to the matter in hand, that, in striving after the contemplation of the truth, we should not only not be deceived by the name of Christ, by means of those who have the name and have not the deeds; but also not by certain deeds and miracles, for when the Lord performed of the same kind for the sake of unbelievers, He has warned us not to be deceived by such things, thinking that an invisible wisdom is present where we see a visible miracle. Hence He annexes the statement: "Many will say to Me on that day, Lord, Lord, have we not prophesied in Thy name, and in Thy name have cast out devils, and in Thy name done many wonderful works? And then will I say[472] unto them, I never knew you: depart from Me, ye that work iniquity." He will not, therefore, recognise any but the man that worketh righteousness. For He forbade also His own disciples themselves to rejoice in such things, viz. that the spirits were subject

---

472 *Dicam*; Vulgate, *confitebor*; Greek, ὁμολογήσω. Meyer says, "It is the conscious dignity of the future Judge of the world." Bengel calls attention to the great power of the word (*magna potestas hujus dicti*). In this action Christ lays the most confident claim to functions not imparted to any human being.

unto them: "But rejoice," says He, "because your names are written in heaven;"[473] I suppose, in that city of Jerusalem which is in heaven, in which only the righteous and holy shall reign. "Know ye not," says the apostle, "that the unrighteous shall not inherit the kingdom of God?"[474]

But perhaps some one may say that the unrighteous cannot perform those visible miracles, and may believe rather that those parties are telling a lie, who will be found saying, "We have prophesied in Thy name, and have cast out devils in Thy name, and have done many wonderful works." Let him therefore read what great things the magi of the Egyptians did who resisted Moses, the servant of God;[475] or if he will not read this, because they did not do them in the name of Christ, let him read what the Lord Himself says of the false prophets, speaking thus: "Then, if any man shall say unto you, Lo, here is Christ, or there; believe it not. For there shall arise false Christs, and false prophets, and shall show great signs and wonders, insomuch that

---

[473] Luke x. 20.
[474] 1 Cor. vi. 9.
[475] Exod. vii. 0, Exod. viii. 0.

the very elect shall be deceived.[476] Behold, I have told you before."[477]

How much need, therefore, is there of the pure and single eye, in order that the way of wisdom may be found, against which there is the clamour of so great deceptions and errors on the part of wicked and perverse men, to escape from all of which is indeed to arrive at the most certain peace, and the immoveable stability of wisdom! For it is greatly to be feared, lest, by eagerness in quarrelling and controversy, one should not see what can be seen by few, that small is the disturbance of gainsayers, unless one also disturbs himself. And in this direction, too, runs that statement of the apostle: "And the servant of the Lord must not strive; but be gentle[478] unto all men, apt to teach, patient, in meekness instructing those that think differently;[479] if God peradventure will give them repentance to the acknowledging of the truth."[480] "Blessed," therefore, "are

---

476 *Inducantur etiam electi*; Vulgate, *inducantur, si fieri potest, etiam electi.*

477 Matt. xxiv. 23-25.

478 *Mitem…diversa sentientes*; Vulgate, *mansuetum…resistunt veritati.*

479 *Mitem…diversa sentientes*; Vulgate, *mansuetum…resistunt veritati.*

480 2 Tim. ii. 24, 25.

the peacemakers: for they shall be called the children of God."[481]

Hence we must take special notice how terribly the conclusion of the whole sermon is introduced: "Therefore, whosoever heareth these sayings of Mine, and doeth them, is like[482] unto a wise man, which built his house upon the rock." For no one confirms what he hears or understands, unless by doing. And if Christ is the rock, as many Scripture testimonies proclaim[483] that man builds in Christ who does what he hears from Him. "The rain descended, and the floods came, and the winds blew, and beat[484] upon that house; and it fell not: for it was founded upon a rock." Such an one, therefore, is not afraid of any gloomy superstitions (for what else is understood by rain, when it is put in the sense of anything bad?), or of turnouts of men, which I think are compared to winds; or of the river of this life, as it were flowing over the earth in carnal lusts. For

481 Matt. v. 9.
482 *Similis est...*; Vulgate, *assimilabitur*. Meyer, Tholuck, etc, refer this to the future judgment, "I will make him like," etc., when Christ will establish those who keep His sayings for ever (opposed by Alford etc.).
483 1 Cor. x. 4. So Alford, who thinks this signification too plain to be overlooked.
484 *Offenderunt*; Vulgate, *irruerunt*.

it is the man who is seduced by the prosperity that is
broken down by the adversities arising from these three
things; none of which is feared by him who has his
house founded upon a rock, *i.e.* who not only hears,
but also does, the Lord's commands. And the man who
hears and does them not is in dangerous proximity to
all these, for he has no stable foundation; but by hearing and not doing, he builds a ruin. For He goes on to
say: "And every one that heareth these sayings of Mine,
and doeth them not, shall be like unto a foolish man,
which built his house upon the sand:[485] and the rain
descended, and the floods came, and the winds blew,
and beat[486] upon that house; and it fell: and great was[487]
the fall of it. And it came to pass, when Jesus had ended
these sayings, the people were astonished at His doctrine: for He taught them as one having authority, and
not as their scribes."[488] This is what I said before was

---

485 The transitory teachings and institutions of men as opposed
to Christ's own word.

486 *Offenderunt*; Vulgate, *irruerunt*.

487 *Facta est*; Vulgate, *fuit*.

488 Vulgate adds *et Pharisæi*. The people were astonished, not
merely at His teachings, but the dignity and self-consciousness
with which Christ uttered them, *quod nova quædam majestas et
insueta hominum mentes ad se raperet* (Calvin). The Scribes spoke
as expounders of the law, and referred back to Moses for their